Conservation of Manuscripts

Conservation of Manuscripts

A.S. Bisht

AGAM KALA PRAKASHAN
DELHI-52

First Published 2011

ISBN : 978-81-7320-108-0

Published by:
Dr. Agam Prasad, M.A., Ph.D., Diploma in Museology
For Agam Kala Prakashan
34, Central Market, Ashok Vihar
Delhi - 110 052
Tel.: 011-27212195, 65688806-7
Fax: 91-11-27212195
Email: agambooks@gmail.com, info@agamkala.com
www.agamkala.com

Composed by:
Aman Printographics
Delhi - 110 052
Mobile: 9891395309

Printed by:
Chawla Offsets
Delhi-110 052

Printed in India

DEDICATED
WITH LOVE AND DEVOTION
TO
BHAGAWAN SRI SATHYA SAI BABA

PREFACE

I dedicate this attempt to BHAGWAN SRI SATHYA SAI BABA, who I am sure, has charged my battery and energized me to scribble the text of this attempt after He cured me since SAI BABA whom I adore as LIVING GOD, has said on many occasions that" Doctors treat but I cure". After curing me, I had his *Darshan* during His last visit to Delhi and NCR early this year. Incidentally, when I was confined to bed rest, I prayed to Swami please call me to the Prasanthi Nilayam, the abode of supreme peace along with the Delhi *Seva Dal* in Aug. 2010,and I was in Puttaparthi.

This attempt has a special significance since it induced me to go through BABA"S views on Vedas and many other publications on spiritual knowledge published with explanations and commentaries such as *Veda Vahini, Upnishad Vahini,* and many other *vahinis*. He has referred to them being a part of the ancient Indian Culture(*Sanskriti*) based on human values of *Sathya, Dharma, Shanti, Prema and Ahimsha.*This is why He has incarnated once again in India and thanks to Baba having taken me in his fold and shower this most needed Grace to use it in this attempt after my long illness.

Earlier I have dealt with a few different types of artifacts, related to the different materials, their creation by the artists and their conservation/ preservation. I feel that spirituality is supreme, knowledge which includes science and culture which are the two sides of the same coin and hence it was ventured how our ancient texts originated and came directly from the God through oral (*Shruti*) to our great Seers. I consider myself fortunate to have dealt only a fraction of this aspect with love and devotion from the core of my heart. I feel that it was my duty to pass every bit of the practical experience that has been acquired by me by this grace but had no time to use my notes made for the several decades over the years while in service. With the grace of God, some of us of this noble profession of Preservation of our great culture would share this with me in times to come after, especially am gone to merge in Baba. Baba gave me a fresh lease of life for some years as bonus. I leave it to Him because He only knows what is good and what is not so good for me. Here after I want to dedicate all my future writings to Him. Baba often says that science and spirituality complement each other. After retirement Bhagwan gave me a chance to speak to students of schools & collages on moral education, which who enlightened me also through his Educare programmes.

Baba has told in His discourses, time and again that "Duty is God; Work is worship". I believe, when one does his duty to the best of his ability and skill and passes it on to the society, which are our limbs, one has worshiped God and He would be certainly pleased by this act of service which pleases Him most. All faiths, all religions, all disciplines have the Veda as their basis. Practical knowledge is great and it has to be earned the hard way. Some are very good in either the theoretical aspects of Conservation or some are very best in practical Conservation and but some are masters of both. That is what is needed to be a good person first and a top class Conservation Scientist.

I recall that I have made extensive notes and maintained them during my Postgraduate study in Australia and U.S.A. in 1960-61 and 1982-1983, respectively which I am able to use them now besides my lectures on plastic sheets, power point presentation to my students in the NMI, NM, VMH and where ever I was invited for lectures during my long journey from 1991 to 2011, I thank the various persons, especially their authorities with whom, I had chance to learn and then passing on to my students. I acknowledge their help from the core of my heart.

I thank the authorities of the National Museum Institute and it's parent body the National Museum for giving me this chance to share with others and my students whatever little I had experienced during my this long exposure when I was in government service from the year 1954 to 1991 and later for the last twenty years to invite me as a great gesture having given this chance of continuous lecturing the students of their faculty of conservation. I thankfully acknowledge their help and the photographs & slides used by me. I am greatly indebted to Dr. Kamal K. Jain, the Head of the Conservation faculty, NMI who had gone back to RCL Mysore as Project officer of this unit of the NRLC, Lucknow and Shri S.P. Singh Director of Conservation, NM who has retired now from the post of the recently, for keeping me busy even at this advanced age of 78 years including Dr. I.K. Bhatnagar, Dr. M.V. Nair besides Dr. K. K. Jain and other officers of the NMI and NM for encouragement extended to me & all others mentioned in the Bibliography, where ever they are.

Dr. M.V. Nair has again taken over the Head of the conservation faculty of the NMI and has continued to keep me as a senior guest faculty on the NMI, New Delhi. In the last but not the least I am thankful to my friend Dr. Agam Prasad, of Agam Kala Prakashan, Delhi-110052 and his staff members for helping me to see one more also book published by them. I am thankful to my family members for smooth bringing out of this 7th book which has been authored by me and the latest one to be out of press soon for use by my students and colleagues in the various cultural institutions.I leave my further attempts to God.

A.S.Bisht

Makar Sankranti
14 January 2011

LIST OF ILLUSTRATIONS

CONTENTS

Chapter One

INTRODUCTION

In India the tradition of communication of the spiritual knowledge was earlier oral and scholars learnt them by heart by repetition several times. These were thus passed on from one generation to another till they found a method of recording/writing them in physical form. Thus India has one of the oldest traditions and may have the largest collections of manuscripts even though a large chunk of them may have been lost for posterity due to one reason or the other. We find them in different languages and scripts, written on different materials. Manuscript tradition in India also has an illustrious history like the other art forms starting from our ancient texts *Vedas, Upanishads, Puranas, Vadanta, Sastras, Ramayana, Bhagwat Gita* etc. which in those ancient times I agree were first in the form of '*Sruti, the eternal echoes' which were* intangible at that point in time but later became tangible by *Smriti*, as embodied in the words of Manu Yajnavalkya & other writers when the scripts and materials for writing were known with the development of the human civilizations. Iswara and the Vedas have, therefore, coexisted which are *Anantham*, and would remain even of we forgot them.

The word Veda means wisdom, knowledge or vision, and it manifests the *Srutis* from the God in human speech from the breath of *Iswara-*

Nishwartham which was revealed to the sages (*Rishis*) Saints or seers by God himself to a few noble deserving/worthy few souls. The method of Bhakti is given in the Vedas, which speak also of things that have to be avoided. The Vedas lay down the lines of the conduct, the method of living and the ideals to be followed. Vedas are difficult to date because these were passed on orally for about a thousand years before they were written down. Veda described the Divine as subtler than the subtlerst atom and vaster than the vastest object.

According to a vedic scholar Shri Janak Singh cited in the bibliography the first three Vedas were in the form, language and contents . He says that the laws of the Vedas regulate the social, legal, domestic and religious customs of the Indians particularly Hindus to the present day. All the obligatory duties of the Hindus at birth, marriage, death etc. owe their allegiance to the vedic rituals. They draw forth the thought of successive generations of thinkers and so contain within them the different strata of thought. Even though the Vedas originally were the ancient divine revelations but are reported to have been modified in the recent dark age of *Kaliyuga* in which moral values degraded, as we see things in a very bad shape today. The morality in every sphere of life has degraded so low that only God (*Avatar*) can save them now from the doom's day (*Jalpralay*). As a God loving person I feel that these ancient codes of conduct were the best available source of knowledge but the ethical doctrines seem to have been improved from the ancient hymns to the mystical *Upanishads* say that the basic cause of the universeis called as 'Brahman' the one who is Omniscient, Omnipotent and Omnipresent and, therefore, feel that we must preserve them for posterity so that every one lives in peace and harmony and let others also live in peace and enjoy spiritual prosperity. Hi is the ultimate goal of all of us.

As this knowledge was passed on from the Head *Acharya/Guru* of the *Gurukul* or the Head of a Monastery (Head Monk) or the *Mathadhish* of a *Matha* or a Temple Head Priest or in a Satra the *Satradhikari* to the students or pupils who were continuously reciting the slokas, hymes and text, line by line several times, thus learning them by heart. I also recall that during my childhood in a village primary school near my native village in Uttrakhand all students of my age learnt them by heart by *smriti.*

Even the tables of multiplication (*Paharas*) 2 ones are 2, 2, twos are 4 (four) 2 three are 6 and so on after continuously repeating them again and again with my classmates in those olden days in the Dev Bhumi (Uttrakhand).I was in Sikkim in the year 1971 and visited the Institute of Tibetology where I witnessed that the old manuscripts which had decayed were being copied in a fresh paper brought by the monks from Tibet in order to preserve the text in them. This is an ancient method of preservation from Tibet according my personal experience. In Manipur also I am told that copying is being practiced by the cultural institutions where they have employed artists called Likharu or likhaka in Assamese society under the management of the Ahom government attached to the Secretariat whose duty is to copy the manuscripts. The Archive in Manipur are practicing this tradition. Most of these practices, though have some relationship with ***Sanatan Dharm (eternal universal religion)*** are specifically connected with the *Vedic Dharma* belonging to *Adikala- Sanatan* meaning (No knowledge about its beginning or its middle or end).

Bhartiya Sanskriti *is* actually the source of information and education as religious texts in earlier period and were not just for praying to God, but much more than that such as *ayurveda*, astronomy, *arthasastra,* history, philosophy, science and sociology etc. Sathya Sai Speaks (Vol.vii, p.299) and (Sanathana Sarathi, July 2000, pp.193-210) which came as revelations from '***Sri mukh***' of Sai Baba and I quote here. He says that" You should try to follow the noble path laid down by the Vedas. The sacred Vedas, which were handed down to us by our great ancient sages, ensure the welfare of the whole world "*Samasta Lokah Sukhino Bhawantu*". They bestow peace and happiness upon the entire mankind. The Vedas teach us that the Divinity exists in the world as sugar exists in syrup. You cannot see sugar in the syrup but it is there as the inherent sweetness. Similarly God manifests Himself in the world. He said that the lord, God revealed the story of Satyakama while returning from the forest where his Guru, Rishi Gautam had deputed him to look after the ashram caws for garazing for four nights on their way back stayed in four villages and every night one Veda was narrated by the God Himself. He thus became a master of all these four *Vedas*. His face shone with a strange splendor, since *Vedic* illumination had been imparted to him by no less a teacher than the Lord of the Gods Himself. This is how these came directly from the '*sri mukh*' of our ancient *Rishis* who attained (*Jnanam*) knowledge of *Brahma* from *Parabrahm* Himself or from other God and Goddesses in the Vedic age such as the great Sage ***Veda Vyasa***. The date assigned to *Rig-Veda* varied from 4500 B.C. (Max Muller). Modern scholers assign the vedic period from 700 B.C. - 600 BC. However, Bal Gangadhar Tilak assigned thm to 1900 B.C. Upanishads acording to him belong to the period 2500 B.C. - 2000 B.C. They also give fairly good idea about the Vedic Society which existed during the period of Upanishads from Gandhara (Afganistan) which included several kingdoms like Madre (Sailkot) Kuru (Delhi), Kedkya Punjab, Pancala (Kanauj) Kosala (Ayodhya), Videha (Tirhut), Kaushambhi (Kosam in U.P. and Kasi). These area were ruled by Kshatriyas. They shattered learned Berchmans & sages who formulated *Varna* System which is still in vougue. There is however, no agreement on the dates, These dates are their own as assumptions and does not have scientific basis at present.

HISTORY OF WRITING MATERIALS

When the historians read the documents, texts and maps from the past they have to be sensitive to the different historical backgrounds-the context in which the information about the past was produced. As a person working in this field, I feel some continuity in the sources used by scholars who rely on the physical evidences in the form of coins, clay tablets, rock edicts, inscriptions and textual records on Papyrus Birch Bark, Palm Leaf and, Sanchi pat etc. for information. But almost all scholars feel that there are some gaps resulting into discontinuity also. In the recent past the number of such textual documents and records have increased in number as these were scattered every where and are now in the collections. There number has certainly increased with the introduction of paper in our country. Parchment is reported to be more durable than leather in many respects and before the advent of paper various other materials were also used as medium for writing by the Babylonians, papyrus was used by the Egyptians, inscribed clay seals were used by the people of Harappa in India during Indus valley civilization in the undivided India during 3rd millennium B.C., Upanishad denote the study and practice of the innate truth, '*Brahmavidya*', denotes the supremacy of the spiritual contemplation. Silk and strips of wood were used in China, Clay tablets, metal plates, barks & leaves of trees such as palm leaf, birch bark, *Sanchi-pat,* or *Hansi Paat, Tula-pat* have been used in North East India and South East Asia. *Paat* in Assamese refers to Agar tree leaves and term '***pat/paat***' in Assamese means sheet. In Africa, early America and Europe Parchment and vellum were used. All these writing materials were mostly used prior to the so called paper age.

After the invention of paper which is the most fascinating writing material and which could not be replaced with any other medium for a long period of time. However, the past-paper age has witnessed with the advancement of technology as a variety of writing media/informations which could be stored on modern materials such as magnetic media, film media, electronic, optical, digitization and web media, which are in use in the modern world even though paper still remains a preferred material due to it's different varieties which are available of it even to-day. Men of the bygone days have expressed their views on varied subjects by taking help of various materials that have been used through the ages for recording the documentary heritage textual & graphic information such as scrolls of leather. According to some Indian Scholars and Archaeologists, in a seminar of the Indian History and Cultural society held in Faizabad in October, 1992 that the tradition of writing started only from the fourth century B.C. on wards, but according to a popular belief the Vedas are called *(Apourusheya)* not of human origin and are *(Anaaadi)* without a beginning in terms of time.

It is reported that Om, the primordial sound is the *Pranava Nada,* from which all Vedas emerged which teach us the principals of oneness of all living beings (*Aiko Aham Bahushyami*), I was one and willed to be many. Veda means wisdom, knowledge or vision, and it manifests the language of the God in human speech as revealed by the Rishis or Seers. The *Rig Veda* is a Veda full of prayers to Gods for realizing aim of life: the *Yajur Veda* describes the ceremonial and ritual aspects of worship: the *Sam veda* extols the Gods through song and poetry: the *Atharva Veda* gives secret formulae for preserving health and security of body and community. He thus became the master of all the Vedas. This is how these came directly from the *Srimukh* of our *Rishies* who attained the *Brahmagyan* from God the Almighty Himself in the vedic age. According to Scholars the Vedas are difficult to date, because they were passed on orally for about 1000 years or more before these were written down in old Sanskrit. These are in different languages and scripts showing integrity of India and it's diversity of people. They are housed in the various libraries, museums, *madrasas, satras,* monasteries, *muttas* and individuals all over this great country of ours. As regards, skin as a writing surface was reported to have been used in Egypt (2700-2500 BC) because of it's superior handling qualities and durability of the sacred documents. Leather and parchment gained wide acceptance as they possess distinct advantages over alternate materials. Flexibility and lightness of the writing surface were some of the advantages which made their handling easy.

Their surface could easily take up inks and colours besides these could be written on both the sides of it. Erasing and corrections could be easily made so that illuminated manuscripts became possible. They also made stitching easy and book produced in Egypt in 1500 BC, has painting on the surface of the leather, besides papyrus and parchment. Leather was a favorite medium for decorative art. Leather was also used to cover the books for making them decorative after binding them in volumes. Various sources of it were from sheep skin, deer skin or skins of smaller animals and popularly known as parchment. Calf skin on the other hand is known as Vellum. In India we have Mogul period *Charbas* which are very near to vellum and are thin. These have been used for making drawings of the miniatures. Chemically it is collagen, it is also known as polypeptides. Papyrus (Cyperus papyrus-Linn) which comes from the papyrus plant has been one of the earliest writing materials first used in Egypt in the third millennium B.C. up to the eleventh century A.D. It was cultivated in abundance, in the delta of the great Nile river in Egypt. Incidences of the reign of Egyptian Emperor are recorded on papyrus. One of this roll is now preserved in the British Museum Library, London. The writing on papyrus was done with the help of soft brush. Normally carbon ink or ink made of iron salt was used for writing on this medium which gives a permanent writing. In Africa, early America and Europe, Parchment and vellum were used. Parchment & vellum were also used as writing material due to their very smooth surface. In India some of the writing materials and their sources are described here which speak of the wide variety of materials. Today in the age of Multi media we find the information technology increasing many fold, and, therefore, we have to plan our preservation resources according to the increased need by using and taking advantage of the technology now available.

Chapter Two

MATERIALS FOR WRITING

Various materials which were very near to the dwelling units of our ansesters were explored by them and, therefore, studied their usefulness as a writing material. Invention of Iron and the advancement in it's metallurgy brought implements for cutting trees and removal of their bark.

1. BIRCH BARK

Bhojapatra (Betula utilis) a plant product was one of the most popular material used for writing purpose in ancient India, before the invention of paper. The naturally occurring, inner bark of this tree was used for writing. There are four varieties of birch bark available e.g. (i) Yellow birch (Betula luta) mostly grown in New England to georgia, (ii) Black birch (Betula lenta) restricted distribution, (iii) White birch or paper birch (Betula payrifera) north eastern US accros Canada and (iv) Himalayan Silver birch (Betula utilis) in Himalayas. It is slowly dried, oil is applied on the surface, and polishing is done by rubbing with a Polishing Stone to make it smooth. The sheets are then cut according to the required size. It peels off in thin layers and is flexible like paper consisting of cellulose and lignin with natural gums and essential oils.

Inner bark is used for writing purposes and it's lignified tissue constitutes 20.3% of the whole and is known as sclerenchymatous tissue. It can take up ink as in paper. It contains birch oil which has Methyl salicylate acting as a preservative. It imparts a fragrant odour and makes it durable. In Russia books bound in Russian leather do not become mouldy and prevent mouldiness in books bound in leathers which come in contact with it. In India, holes are pierced in the center of the birch bark sheet for a cord to pass through it to keep them together before wrapping them between two wooden covers. Insect repellent is an important property of birch bark. Fungus cannot attack the birch bark easily. In spite of that, aging affects it. In many old houses in Kashmir and also in the Himalayan reign of Uttarakhand we find religious books written in *Prakrit, Pali and* old Sanskrit respectively. It was mainly used in the northern India due to it's easy availability. The main attempt of the Conservation Scientists in India has been to understand the material of the birch bark after necessary scientific study (D.G. Suryawanshi of NRLC for his Ph.D under the guidance of Dr. O.P. Agrawal) so that the decay aspect could be analyzed to know the possible cause of their decay. I was outside Examiner for his Thesis. The birch bark is composed of the inner bark of the tree Birch *(Betula utilis)* which when studied in detail comprise of several thin layers.

There is a natural adhesive in between the layers initially which looses the adhesion power with time of sticking the sheets together, resulting in brittleness and consequent loss of physical strength due to aging and handling. Birch–bark (bhogi- patra or bhurja- patra) was one of the main materials used in India for writing since 2nd or 3rd century A.D. It is in fragments that describe *Dhammapada* and is written with black ink in *kharosti* script. Birch- bark is composed of several layers, each of which is very thin almost like a tissue – paper. It normally has a very light streak of brown colour on one side and brownish white on the other. The layers are joined together by a natural gum and woody knots and streaks which are composite part of the bark. It becomes weak and fragile making them difficult to handle since they loose their flexibility.

2. PALM LEAVES

Palm leaves were one of the main support used for writing manuscripts particularly in south and south – east Asian countries including India, Nepal, Sri Lanka, Burma and Indonesia etc. It's use was very popular during 17th to 20th century A.D.. It is reported that palm leaf was being used liberally for writing purposes and we get palm leaf manuscripts till 11th-12th cent. but only very few examples have survived due to the adverse climatic conditions in this part of the world. There are many varieties of leaves of the Palm – tree. which are used for the writing purpose (a) Sri Tal (Corypha umbraculifera) (b) Tad or Tadd palmyra palm (Borassus flabellifer). Of these the former *Sri-talam* gives leaves that are smooth and supple. The elasticity and flexibility of the leaves allow them to be bent to a considerable extent. The *tad* leaves on the other hand are thick, hard and non-elastic. They have a tendency to break easily. There is a lot of difference in their quality.

There were two different methods of writing on palm leaves. Tad leaves are cut, trimmed to size and treated with lime water. On drying were oiled with Gingeli oil (Til oil) and were written with a pointed stylus made of iron to incise letters and illustrations into the body of the leaves. The leaves were then rubbed with lamp black or charcoal powder or carbon black. Line drawings were incised with a pointed stylus and smeared with charcoal. Some time the sheets are stitched edge to edge together to get the required size. The other method to write on sri tala is the use of pen and ink to write, illustrations, monochrome as well as polychrome, were done with a brush as in case of a painting. For this process, first an outline was drawn with black ink and then the paints are filled in on a ground as in case of a miniature which was laid earlier.

3. SANCHI-PAT

Sanchi-pat is made from the bark of the Agar or Aloe tree (Acquilaria agallocha) and is the most common carrier for manuscripts of Assam. *Tula-pat* is mostly made by *Ahoms and others of Shan* extraction. Tangible aspect says it is a plant product so the knowledge of science to be utilized to preserve them were there even in 7th cent. AD. Intangible aspect says of their worship as *EK Sarnia* (Devotion to Sole Almighty) Lord Vishnu or Krishna. Lord krishna to be worshiped through *Nam Prasanga* or fourteen prayers instead of a statue in the shrine. Though manuscript tradition prevailed in Assam since quite an earlier age, it attainted its zenith from 15th cent. A.D. onwards during neo-*Vaisnavite* movement under *Srimanta Sankardeva* (1449-1568 A.D.) and his disciple Madhadev started this cult.

I got a chance to examine a large number of these manuscripts stored in the *Vaisnavite Satras* resembling Buddhist Monasteries, where these are worshiped in place of an image. Lord Krishna, unlike in Hindu temples, in other parts of India, where Idol is worshiped but in these *Satras Puthi* of *Bhagwat* is kept in the Centrum sanctorum for worship. The *Satras* are still the living cultural centers with regular activities including music, dance, drama and total learning. These are the centers of learning, hearing, *kirtan* and *Nama sranwan* in the Prayer hall within the premises of a *Satra*. Majuli is the largest river island in the world in *Brahmaputra* which contains 66 *Satras* of which *Auni Satra,* is the largest and the oldest. Culturally rich Majuli has a rich tradition of Assam and has a unique traditional technique of making *Sanchi paat* manuscripts. It is on the River *Brahma-putra,* which means son the only male river in India where as most of the other rivers in India are female.

Agar bark (Aquilaria agallacha) *Sanch-pat* or Hansi Pat which consists of cellulose and lignin. It absorbs ink just like sri tala. Sheets are dried for many days before curing, seasoning and polishing. This is followed by treatment with Orpiment to make them immune from insects and rubbing them with a conch shell to make it smooth. Painting is done by using both organic and inorganic colours. Carbon as well as Iron gall ink are used as per requirement of the manuscript besides a special ink called 'Sanchi Mahi'.

Palm leaf and *Tengna*, a local plant from Manipur, are also lignified cellulose, whose leaves resemble palm leaves and were also used for writing manuscripts in Manipur. These are kept in a Kitchen and smoking helps in their preservstion. It contains essential oils also. Colours are mostly organic, besides lac, soot and '*UTI MACHI* 'a local name. Writings have a glaze/ shine. It seems to have been in a way influenced by the neighboring country Myanmar (Burma) and at times by China as well. Later after the advent of paper, Manipur also started making paper by hand.

4. PAPER

(a) Ancient Paper

The credit for the invention of paper goes to a Chinese, Ts'ai Lun in 105 A.D. Some scholars say that paper was first made in India as there is a reference of paper making in India in 'Indica' authored by Niorchus, a representative of Alexander the great, in Punjab, around 327 B.C.. Megasthenes, in the court of Chandragupta Maurya in 306 B.C .had also mentioned that Indian people used paper in small scale as 'Kagad' or 'kadgal' before the Chinese. This aspect needs further study to come to some conclusive fact. Before invention of paper Chinese used wood, bamboo strips and silk, etc. for writing purposes as they used these materials continuously for many centuries. An account of making various kinds of paper would be discussed later keeping it's importance in mind.

According to a rough estimate there are many lakhs of manuscripts in Sanscrit, Prakrit, Pali and many other south Indian languages from the various parts of the country. It is also a fact that a large number of Indian ancient manuscripts are now in countries abroad. I remember that one of my colleagues who was in the Manuscript department of the National Museum and was an expert of *Sharda* manuscripts on Birch bark migrated to the West Germany. Chinese Ink was being made by grinding of soot in water and glue. Today paper is the main material used for writing but many scholars abroad say it's origin is not in India. In India, however, the technique of paper making was acquired as early as 327 B.C.. In the accidental origin paper was made from cotton and linen rags or mixture of these fibers. But the production was so little that it became difficult for the paper makers to cope with the growing demand of the 18th century.

Paper word derives its origin from the word 'papyrus' (earlier mentioned). The earliest evidence of papyri has been dated to 3500 B.C. Papyrus existed as the main civilized writing material at least about 4000 year back. The history of the development of paper is interesting and more so because some of its basic steps in its processing have not yet changed. Parchment the second source of writing purpose was introduced in or about 170 BC. It was recognized as a substitute of papyrus. Parchment had the advantage of being more durable than papyrus, Egyptian ink was reported to have been prepared by mixing carbon black mixed with oil to protect it from the relatively damp Mediterranean climate.

According to Forbes, during the early middle ages in Europe, the best parchment was made from the skin of unborn lambs or calves. Later on bamboo strips were substituted with woven materials. They made scroll of woven textiles to write upon. But the textile material suffered heavy losses due to unnecessary wastage taking place in the scrolling process. In due course of time, however, they thought over to utilize this waste, by beating the discarded cloth and separating them into fiber form. This fibrous material after squeezing the extra water was transformed into sheets. The sheet so prepared was dried and used for writing purpose. The Chinese nationals kept to themselves the secret of the art of paper making for almost five centuries then, to exercise a monopoly over the art.

After this the Arabs got this art of paper making when they repelled the invasion on Samarkand. Arab generals persuaded the invaders and took some Chinese prisoners. From these prisoners Arabians learnt to make paper. Later on the art of paper making was brought to Japan by a Buddhist monk Dokyo in 610A.D. through Korea, so this art spread to central Asia and Europe. Spain manufactured first paper in 1055 A.D. The route of transmission of paper making technique is described in various Chinese version as stated above

(b) Modern Paper

Drawing paper is strong, well-sized paper, is used for making drawing formerly it used to be made from rags but today it is usually made from chemically refined pulp to which rags (now usually textile scraps) are sometimes added; Glazed paper can be compressed and glazed by pressure between the rollers if a calendar according to the degree of gloss glazed paper is termed hot pressed or not hot pressed the latter is known as cold pressed in America paper that has not been glazed is known as rough. Impregnated paper is dipped into solutions of impregnation agents in order to endow it with certain properties: wax paper is waterproof; silicone paper is hydrophobic; there is paper that does not ignite easily, and paper that is resistant to attack by micro-organisms.

Handmade paper is also known as vat paper that is to say paper removed from the vat by hand A characteristic of handmade paper is the deckle edge that forms along the inner edge with irregular edges is today sometimes also called deckle-edged; deckle edges closely resembling those of handmade paper can be made on the cylinder mould machine imitation deckle edges made with irregularly serrated knives are barely distinguishable from "genuine" deckle edged. Deckle-edged paper is generally made from constituents that ensure its high quality. In addition to having size added to its pulp, it is usually surface-sized.

Works of Art on Modern Paper are such as Lithographs, Etching, Engraving and Water colour to mention a few. Lithograph is a print produced by Lithography which is an art or process of making a print using greasy ink or Crayon on porus stone (Lime stone) or roller which has been treated to accept in ink only where it is required for printing. Lithgraphic printing. Photo lithography is called litho print. It was introduced in Germany by Aloys Senefalder in 1798. In it the person who draws it differs from who has printed it. Etching consists of drawing with fine steel point or needle on a soot blackened metal plate which has been coated with a ground acid resisting wax or varnish. The first dated etching is of 1513 AD.

In other words it is a copy or representation produced by the process of etching; an impression from an etched plate. An etching ground is prepared with a protective substance with which a surface is coated preparatory to etching. Here also the person who has drawn it would differ from the one who has engraved it. From 16th cent. AD onwards, the Portugusse, Duch, English, Danish and French established trading settlements etc. around coastal India important of which were Madras (Chennai), Bombay (Mumbai) and Cacutta (Kolkata). Professional portrait and landscape painters as well as Engravers began to arrive with permission from the East India company from 1760 A.D. onwards. The heyday of artistic activity among British artists in India is considered with the golden age of engraving and lithography in the 18th and 19th cent.

Engravings drawn and engraved by Daniell brothers (Thomas and Williams), Kolkata are predominantly available in various collections of institutions like the Victoria Memorial Hall, Kolkata or Fort Saint George Chennai etc. besides various government houses, Raj Bhavans, Rashtrapati Bhavan which depict India of that period artistically are very important in the Indian history of that period. These prints have been given the tonal gradation of colours by the technique of 'aquatints'. The aquatints as described by Sutton, were used to be done by drawing on wax coated copper plates and then by repeated beatings of the copper plate. Oil Painting by the use of a powdered resin and some acid resistant substance. These were then printed, binding the pigments by use of processed Linseed oil (to better drying substance). Water colour is a painting done in water soluble medium making the colours to be absorbed by paper support and the paint layer is very thin as compared to miniatures.

(c) *Manufacture of Paper and it's Demand*

Gradually paper manufactures took to advertising for collecting rags in exchange of story books, candles, rings etc. The paper manufactures started selling the paper by weight. They put loading material was introduced in paper. Various raw materials such as bamboo (*bans*) jute (*tat*) flax (*san*) were used for making paper. Paper was also produced from water silk cocoons; since it cracks it was not used by Painters. The various centers of paper manufacture, by the 16th century, started producing excellent paper of thick and durable variety capable of being highly burnished and decorated.

The best paper however, came from Kalpi (U.P.) and was manufactured from the old nets of fisherman and hence called *mahajala*. Such a paper had always been white in colour, flax obtained form finishing nets was perfectly bleached in water. Till the 18th century the production centers and methods of manufacturing paper for Muslims and Hindu manuscripts were different, Hindu paper making was apparently much more localized and the sheets of paper produced were much smaller in size, normally to the size of a folio required for a manuscript. The larger sheets were favored in the Muslims centers and were cut into required sizes. Paper making was considered to be one of the premier cottage industries before the commencement of the British rule in India.

Asrarul-khat a 17th cent. text in the collection of the National Museum, New Delhi describes various types of papers being manufactured in India. The first paper factory was started in Bengal in the latter half of 18th century AD by a Christian missionary. The hundred years that followed never saw the foundation of another such industry. It was only in 1867 A.D. that a real beginning was made and a modern paper mill was established at Bali near Kolkata in Bengal. Paper played a very important role in our civilized society. By the 16th cent. many centers of paper manufacture came to be established. For this process the chief raw materials used for the manufacture of paper were bamboo, jute, flax, cotton, old discarded fishing nets, it was very white because of the flax obtained from it was perfectly bleached. The chief centers were Daulatabadi, Nizamabad, Kalpi, Patna, Sanganer, Kashmir, Sialkot, etc.

Paper is a substance made in the form of sheets or leaves from rags, straw, bark, wood or other fibrous material for various use. Exparto grass was used in 1861 A.D.. Chemical and Mechanical wood pulp were used in 1880 A.D and 1885 A.D.. A sheet of paper consists chiefly of vegetable fibers of different lengths and sizes twisted and interlaced with each other and finally squeezed together to make a sheet or web with a suitable surface for writing or printing. Paper is an inter-laced web of fibers formed by the action of tiling from water suspension which is dried and finished. At present, it is an important means of transmission of thoughts through books, manuscripts, journals and newspapers. Paper requires a specialized knowledge as per its manufacturer. The quality and stability of paper is governed in the first instance by the raw materials from which it is made and different types of cellulose fibers used for paper which consists of a felted mat of natural (mainly cellulose) fibers, and although it might contain sizes, fillers and other additives most of its mechanical strength originates from the physical interlocking of these irregularly surfaced fibers. The strength of paper is determined not so much by the strength of the fibers themselves but by the strength possessed by the linkage will lead directly to a decrease in its durability. Length and arrangement of linear chain of cellulose molecule are discussed later

The raw material for the paper making are numerous in the modern world. Before 19th Century paper making cellulose fibers came from cotton rags, grasses, bamboo, esparto, cereal streams etc. Bast fibers from flax, hemp, jute etc. and seed hairs from cotton were there, since AD 1800. Forest tree trunks were the major sources for cellulose fibers. For improving upon the quality of paper surface which is used today for printing and writing, sizing and loading are two important steps in paper manufacture. Loading materials are inorganic such as China clay, calcium carbonate, talc, asbestos, gypsum, titanium dioxide etc.. Sizing materials are both inorganic and organic such as starch, casein, gelatin, rosin and sodium silicate.

5. INKS IN INDIA

In India some of the writing materials and their sources are described here which speak of the wide variety of materials. Ink is one of the most important elements of a manuscript and to be dealt in detail. The origin of ink followed the invention of the writing material when the practice of this art which had advanced beyond the age of stone inscriptions, rock edicts, clay tablets and wooden plaques etc. besides the reed pen (*Kalam)* and brushes. We may, therefore, link the genesis of ink to 4000 years back from now i.e well before the birth of Christ. It might have been not very difficult to make black/coloured mixtures for this purpose which came from plants or inorganic substances from the earth.

(i) Carbon Inks

Carbon based inks are among the oldest of inks and were perhaps the first to be used about 2000 years back and were made from charcoal powder mixed with water and gum. These were obtained by a process of semi-combustion of organic materials, which were then dispersed in water. Carbon inks are usually made from charcoal soot suspended in a glue or gum medium. In fact most of the quality inks were made from lamp black. The colour varied from dark brown to blue black. Carbon based inks were used in ancient Egypt, China and India .It is permanent and has no adverse effect on the material written upon. Dating of ink can be done on the basis that Iron gall ink was first used in the 12th cent. AD. Indian ink and carbon ink were being used earlier than this century in India.

(ii) China Ink

It is also called as China ink or formerly known by the ancients and classical and later times Indian Ink. This was obtained from soot produced by the smoke of pine and the oil in lamps, mixed with the gelatin of asses skin and musk to improve the odour of oil. This ink is easily washed away unless bichromate of ammonium or potassium in minute quantities is added to it. If the paper is exposed to sunlight for a sort time, gummy compound will be rendered insoluble and can not be removed with any fluid, chemical or otherwise. Metallo-acid inks are very common in manuscript and are characterized by their colour, obtained from a metal to which acid is added as a fixative.

(iii) Iron gall Ink

Iron tannin ink replaced the carbon inks in the middle ages as the general writing fluid because these were easier to handle. Iron gall ink is the most important ink especially in the western history. It has been analyzed and proved that Leonardo da-vinci wrote his notes using Iron gal ink. To make iron gal ink, galls from oak trees were crushed to obtain gallo tanic acid and finally mixed with water to form gallic acid. As the ink is prepared by the reaction of iron with gall solution, it is known as Iron gall ink. For writing purpose carbon ink as well as tannate ink were used.

(iv) Sanchi-mahi

For writing on sanchipat mention of a special kind of ink called Sanchi-mahi was used. The ink used in Assam is of very high quality and can resist very un favourable conditions without fading.It is also reported that the characteristic of Assamese ink is it's tenacity to glossy and slippery surfaces. It's durability has been proved by the old manuscripts whose ink has not faded appreciably. The most commonly used ink in Assam is prepared from *silikha (Terminalia citrina)* mixed with bull's urine or blood of a locally available fish (known as kuchiya). Sometimes iron powder is also used to intensify the ink. Inks and colours were prepared from various indigenous products. A special kind of ink was prepared for writing by boiling burnt almond shells in cow's urine till such times as the urine gets evaporated completely. This ink was said to be indelible and is reported to be insoluble in water.

Inks and colours are also prepared from (a)Amalaka (Phyeanthus amblica), (b)Alandhu (Soot) Lamp black, (c) Keharaj (a kind of dark green creeper) (d)Lacquer (e) Gold (leaf or powder with gum of bhotera), (f)Hengul (g) Haital (h) Khari-mati and sap of earth worm was used as an invisible ink

6. TECNIQUES OF MAKING: MATERIALS SUITABLE FOR WRITING

To prepare Papyrus, as writing material, it is reported that the stem was cut into longitudinal strips those form the center of the plant being the broadest and made them suitable for use. The strips were laid side by side to the required width, thus forming a layer across which another layer of short strips were laid at right angles. The two layers thus woven formed a sheet which was then soaked in water. The sheet was finally hammered and dried in the Sun. Any roughness was leveled by polishing with ivory or a smooth shell to roll.

The birch is a moderately sized, deciduous tree growing at a height of about 4600m in the Himalayas. It was actually the inner bark of the tree which was used for writing. The bark after being peeled off the tree, was dried, oil was then applied over it and it was polished. Finally it was cut to a suitable size strips and kept between two wooden covers for protection. The writing was done on the bark with a very soft brush and *Kalam* using carbon ink.

Writing is made on the palm leaf with sharp metallic needle by scratching/inscribing for convenience in reading carbon black (charcoal powder) mixed with oil is applied on the surface for legibility. To prepare the palm leaves for writing they were first dried after boiling them for a few hours and then these are dried again. When these are completely dry, they are burnished with a stone or conch shell. The leaves are then cut to a required size. According to customs prevailing in south India, fresh Palm leaves were dried in the shade and then gingili oil was applied over their surface to make them smooth in some parts of South India, tender Palm leaves were hung for several days in the kitchen where smoke was emitted. Afterwards they were cleaned and used for writing. This practice is also prevalent in Orissa and some other eastern states of India. Some Orissan people apply turmeric paste to them and the turmeric gives the leaves a light yellow colour. Leaves are dried completely in the sun and are kept under mud or silt of a pond for 10-15 days. Afterwards these are removed, cleaned and dried again in the sun for some time. Finally a paste of turmeric is applied. Orissa use to boil the rough and matured leaves in water for some time. This made the leave thin, soft and then cleaned with soft cloth and kept alternately in cold and hot water.

People of Assam choose the bark (sheet) of the Agar tree. Sanchi-pat for these manuscripts because of it's easy availability very near to the Satras and thus having also associated with the religious sentiments of the devotees dedicated to Lord Krishna. Tula-pat, where as was used for manuscripts and also for making miniatures It is reported that a Tula pat folio was made by stitching two sheets together or by folding a bigger and longer sheet and then stitching them together. Some scholars still describe it to a paper made from wood pulp. Perhaps a detailed scientific study would clarify the position. The wood used has been reported as a specific variety of Mulberry (Bronsanettia spp.).

(a) Composition and Fibre Properties of Materials

Cellulose comprises 60% to 80% of the total solid matter of wood. It is mostly in the form of water insoluble fibers. Fibers from different sources have different physical properties, length, width, wall thickness, cavity, diameter in addition to this varying chemical composition, varying amount of main constituents of wood cellulose, hemicelluloses, lignin and extractives, Rag used for paper making consist almost of cellulose of various chain lengths. A typical wood on the other hand might contain about 29% lignin, 43% cellulose, 27% other carbohydrate material and one percent extractives. These constituents may vary.

The properties of paper depend upon the structure of fibers and the other addition from which it is made, base of the fiber is mainly cellulose. Cellulose is a linear polysaccharide, composed of glucose anhydride units linked together end of end. The total number of glucose units that are joined to form a cellulose molecule is termed "degree of polymerization". Cellulose is in the form of bundles of molecules or fibrils within the fiber wall. It is logical to believe that the structure and properties of paper and their variations can be better understand by having a great knowledge of the properties and interactions of the individual fibers. Investigations recognized the importance of fiber dimensions to the properties of paper i.e fiber length, width, wall thickness, and ratio of fiber to width especially between softwood and hard wood species. During recent years more attention has been given to the mechanical properties of the individual fibers, such as tensile strength, bonding strength, fiber flexibility and collapse and effect of these properties by chemical and mechanical treatment.

(b) Suitability of Raw Material for Paper Making

Wood represents the most important renewable natural resources and the annual growth is sufficient to satisfy many essential needs indefinitely into the future, the major component of wood, cellulose is one of the most abundant naturally occurring organic compound, which is having a indispensable for the field of paper making industries. Cellulose is 50% of the woody structure of the plants. 10% of the dry weight of the leaves and over 98% of the cotton fibers. It is easily accessible, replenishable and easily harvested and transported. It has a great affinity for water which facilitates the mechanical preparation of fiber and fiber to fiber bonding when the fibrous mixture get dry. It is naturally white, it is insoluble in water and neutral organic solvents. Structurally it is a very long chained compound, its structural formula is represented as follows: -

Cellulose : formula $(C_6H_{10}O_5)n$

"HEMICELLULOSES"

It is another term which refers in a loose way to a class of substances rather than to a definite compounds. They may be regarded as complex compounds. They are important constitute of the walls of the fiber cells, and help to "cement" the fibers together. In the cooking condition the degradation of hemi cellulose always takes place. Hemi cellulose are responsible for several important properties of pulp fibers. It improves the flexibility of the fibers by imbibing water.

(c) *Structure of Paper*

The carbohydrates are represented chiefly by the polysaccharides, which account for roughly three fourths of the wood substance. Almost all the carbohydrates in wood are composed of long polymeric chains of an hydro sugar units and that is called polysaccharides. They include cellulose the group of cold-water insoluble non cellulose. Polysaccharides commonly designated as hemicelluloses. Starch and peptic substances they form a partially ordered structure. Lignin is distributed in the structure but is concentrated particularly in the middle that forms lamella the typical intercellular material.

Lignin is the principal constituent other than cellulose of plant materials and which comprises up to 30% of the total plant product. Lignin is distributed in the structure but is concentrated particularly in the middle lamella which forms the typical intercellular material. In spite of several researches the structure of lignin is not known completely. Lignin is the generic term for the non-crystalline complex, aromatic, components, believed to be predominantly polymeric phenol propane type, containing a varying amount of methoxy group liquids which contain minor amount of various aromatic acids. Lignin is the "glue" that holds the fibers of wood together and is present to some extent in the cell walls where it is associated with cellular structure. By means of appropriate colour reactions, lignin has been shown to be present in all vascular plants. In mature plants, stems, roots, barks, leaves, fruit shells and seed hairs are all lignified to varying degrees. The lignified cellulose have been found in the loosening of its lignin content as it bound to decay due to the photochemical degradation which though more prone to decay due to the UV rays which spreads due to the UV radiations a smaller portion of which extends in the visible light portion of the spectrum in to the first few radiations but does not reach up to the last radiation i.e. the red of the visible portion.

1. FABRICATION TECHNIQUES

Wood consists of cellulose, lignin and hemi cellulose (acting as a binding material) waxes, resin and coloured materials. The separations of cellulose from the associated materials from wood can be achieved by chemical or mechanical process.

2. PULPING PROCESS

Paper does not occur in nature as other writing materials. It has to be processed from other materials such as cotton rags, woods and grass etc. which has to under go the processes described here under.

The pulping process is of three types: Mechanical, chemical and semi-mechanical. It is made from either soft or hard wood most important commercial processes are sulphite, sulphate and soda. These chemical treatment dissolves most of the ligneous binding material and permits separations of the cellulose fibers. The pulp is bleached to remove coloured materials and other impurities.

(a) Sulphite Process

Pulp is prepared by cooking wood chips with solution containing calcium bisulphate with an excess of free sulphurous acid (H_2So_3). Other bases such as sodium ammonium and magnesium are being substituted for calcium because of improved product, ease in recovery of inorganic chemicals. Basically sulphur dioxide in the presence of bisulphate salts combine with lignin to form ligneous sulphonate which enters into solution and thus removed.

(b) Alkaline Process

The chips are digested with a solution of caustic soda (Na OH) of about 4% concentration and at the temperature of 170°C to 175°C for 2 hours. The soda process has declined in importance with the growth of the sulphate pulp industry.

(c) Sulphate or Kraft Pulp Process

Sulphate or kraft pulp is made by the digestion of chips with a pulping liquor containing sodium hydroxide and sodium sulphide. The process can be used for pulping almost any fibrous raw materials. Cooking cycle requires about three to four hours at 170° to 175°C temperature.

3. BLEACHING OF CHEMICAL PULP

The pulp produced by any of the common pulping processes contain residual lignin, and caloured materials further purification can be accomplished by bleaching agents such as gas, hypochlorites, chlorine dioxide and peroxides. They are usually applied in several sequences to consume bleaching chemical and to minimize degradation of cellulose in the pulp.

(a) Mechanical Process

Mechanical wood pulp or ground wood is produced by grinding wood against a rotating abrasive stone under a stream of water. Most ground wood is made from soft woods. Ground wood contributes absorbency bulk and opacity of a paper sheet and is lower in cost than chemical pulp. This process does not remove lignin in the pulp.

Chemical ground wood is produced from hard wood by first subjecting the whole logs to a chemical treatment with sodium sulphite and sodium carbonate at elevated temperature and pressure. The log is then reduced to fibers by the grinding process. Bleached ground wood is produced by treatment of mechanical pulp with sodium peroxide, hydrogen peroxide sodium hydro sulphite. The bleached ground woods are used chiefly in book grades.

Fabrication is also best from the other sources than wood. The cotton fibers, rags, bast fibers of hemp, jute and flax can be pulped by cooking with caustic soda. The cooked stock is washed and bleached grasses such as straw esparto, reed and bamboo can be pulped by the soda, kraft or neutral sulphite process.

4. TECHNIQUE OF HAND MADE PAPER

The bast fibers were soaked for a day or were drained and were then boiled in an alkaline solution. The water was drained off and the fibers were beaten with a wooden mallet or by a mortar and pestle. Unbeaten bits were then picked out by hand, and the fibers were stirred into water to turn into a dilute suspension in a tank. Than the whole was bleached by basking in the sun. After wards some of the suspension was dipped into a rectangular mould, fitted at the bottom with a sieve made of bamboo strips. After water had been drained away, the mould and the wet sheet were dried in front of the fire.

Flour and gelatin, rosin from pine and alum were used for sizing papers. At this time paper making industry flourished. The process involved the separation of work. An improvement was made by puffing the sheets between pieces of felt and pressed to squeeze the water, before drying on a heated all coated with lime, instead of drawing the sheet with mould. The production was thus greatly increased. This was the affair before the introduction of the paper machine.

5. MACHINE MADE PAPER

In 1978 the four rainier machine was invented by Nicholas Robert of France and development followed by the four brothers in England. The paper machine ferrous process dries the sheet in one continuous operation. Today except for the making of some special art paper the bulk of paper production is by machine.

6. PROCESS OF PAPER MAKING BY MACHINE

Cellulose fibers are first processed by beating, rinsing in water suspension by mechanical cutting and shearing action in a beater. This leads to fabrication of the fibers. The dilute suspension, usually 0.1 to 0.5% fibers in water, in called the stock. In the foundry machine, the stock is feed from a reservoir called the heard box through a horizontal slot called slice onto an endless moving wire screen. Over is double faced oil cloth apron. The water drains through the wire under the influence of gravity, the web of the heavily formed sheet leaves the wire and is pressed by the press rolls to compact the fiber and to remove additional water. After passage through the press section, the water content of the sweet is reduced to about 65 to 80% from the press section the sheet passes to the dryer section which comprise series of steam – heated cylinders. The paper web is held in contact with each layer by a felt the paper which contains to 10% of moisture. The finished paper is wounded into a large reel at the end of the machine.

The treatment known as calendaring increases the smoothness and gloss of the paper surface. A calendar comprises two or more cast-iron rolls with hardened surface, which are arranged in a set or stock and rest vertically on the other at the end of the dryer section in the paper machine.

7. SIZING

Many types of paper, but writing paper especially, were dipped, sheet by sheet, into solutions of gelatin size or starch paste to decrease the absorbency of the paper and stop ink and colours from running, sizing also increases the strength of the paper. Sized as well as unsized paper had to be smoothened after drying. either by hand with a sleeking-stone or with mechanically – driven sleeking hammer, in later times this was also done in rolling mills. A small paper mill with a vat employed about 10 to 15 people and produce up to 3000 sheets a day, depending on the size of the sheets.

A watermark is produced in hand made paper by forming a raised design on the wire screen when the sheet is made, the pulp is thinned in areas imposed by the designs. The watermarking of paper during manufacturing on a special type machine is accomplished by divvy rolls which has raised pattern corresponding to the dried water mark. As the roll is rotated above the moving wire and in contact with the wet sheet, the design is impressed into the fiber mat and appears as partially transparent area then the paper is dried. Chemical watermarks are made by introducing a agent into the paper to simulate conventional watermark.

8. STUDY OF PAPER

Method for distinguishing hand made and machine made paper

1) Handmade paper tears in the same way in all directions, whereas the machine-made paper tears more easily in the machine direction than in the cross directions.
2) Expansion of hand-made paper upon wetting is the same is all directions, whereas the expansion of machine made paper is greater in the cross direction than the machine direction.
3) On floating a sheet of paper in water machine made paper cockles in the machine directions, while hand made paper in all directions.
4) Hand made paper has natural shrinkage while machine made paper has not.

9. IMPORTANT PROPERTIES OF PAPER

(i) Physical Properties

It includes thickness, weight, density, hardness, stiffness and tensile strength.

(ii) Chemical Properties

Measurement of pH of Paper, determination of moisture content, cellulose, copper number of viscosity.

(iii) Optical properties

It includes light remittance, light absorption and light reflectance.

(iv) Electrical Properties

It includes dielectric strength, specific inductive capacity and electrical conductivity. Some fundamental properties of paper are density, dielectric strength, colour, hardness, light absorption, tensile strength and thickness. The advantage of fundamental test is that once the fundamental characterstic are thoroughly underscored it should be possible to. Some important properties are oftenly used for paper testing, those are permeability to liquid surface bonding, printability and folding endurance. The paper samples should be protected from excess heat, light and not be allowed to come into the contact with the liquids. Paper testing should be carried out in a room maintained at constant temperature (usually 73-3.5°F) and constant relative humidity (usually 50 + 22%) in England and France 65% relative humidity and 65 to 70° F temperature are used. Following above all the properties, it is decided that initial consideration should be given to the physical strength properties for the paper testing to determine the durability of the paper.

The second consideration should be given to the amount of acidity contained in the paper because the acidity is one of the principal causes of deterioration of paper.

10. PHYSICAL PROPERTIES OF PAPER

The Physical strength of paper is commonly measured by tensile stress folding endurance, tearing strength and bursting strength.

(a) Tensile Strength

Tensile strength is the maximum tensile stress developed in a tension test carried to rupture the paper strip under prescribed condition. The tensile stress is measured by a tensile tester strip of a paper of specified length and width are stressed of failure. The tensile strength at failure, the stretch and sometimes the total work to failure are recorded. The stretch is the distance which the paper will stretch before it breaks. Tensile failure occurs primarily because of failure of inter fiber bonds, although observation of tensile break shows that many individual fibers are broken.

(b) Folding endurance

Folding endurance tester mechanically produce double folds repeated at the same point of specimen strips, and subject the strip to tension after each folds. The result is expressed in the number of folds before rupture at the crease, folding endurance has double significance. The test is especially important in papers which are subjected to folding for example recorder papers, map papers, currency paper and bark papers. It is also a sensitive measure of influences tending to degrade fiber, hence is useful to indicate again properties of paper.

(c) Treating strength tester

Treating strength tester is also an important property to test the significance in determining the resistance to rupture of paper by the force in grames. It is a measure of the average force in grams required to tear a single sheet of paper after the tear has started. It has been found that the alkaline cooked pulps have higher tear than corresponding acid cooked pulps. Fiber length and inter fiber bonding are both important factors in tearing strength. Longer fiber improves tear strength.

(d) Bursting strength

Bursting strength is defined as the hydrostatic pressure in PSI required to produce rupture of the material when the pressure is applied at a controlled increasing rate through a rubber diaphragm to a circular area; 1.20 inch Index meter of the material under test. The pressure required to burst the paper is indicated on a tube gauge. Long fibers although beneficial to high bursting strength are of secondary importance to inter fiber bonding.

(e) Chemical Properties

Moisture Content: The comparative strength of paper can be expressed in terms of fiber quality. The most important method are those for cellulose; copper number, and viscosity. Cellulose is a hygroscopic material and under ordinary conditions it holds an amount of water which depends on the temperature and the relative humidity of the surrounding atmosphere. In analysis the moisture content is of concern chiefly in its effect on the weight of dry material in the test sample. For purpose of uniformity and comparison of data it is desirable to report results as a percentage of the moisture free or oven dry material. The analysis of pre dried paper is undesirable for two reason. The analytical values found may be altered if the paper is first dried in the oven and it is difficult to avoid absorption of moisture while weighing a sample of the dried material. Consequently it is customary first to condition the paper until it reaches equilibrium with the air of the laboratory. Then the test sample is weighted and at the same time a separate sample is weighed for moisture determination so that the results of the analysis can be calculated to the oven dry basis. The moisture content is usually expressed as a percentage of the moist material.

There are three principal direct methods for determining the moisture content of paper.

1) Drying in a electrical heated oven at about 100 to 105°C
2) Drying in a vacuum oven which may be operated at a temperature in the range of 60 to 120°C
3) Drying preferably in vacuum oven an efficient desiccant such as phosphoric and dried.

The oven drying method in most commonly used for determining the moisture content of paper.

(f) Cellulose

When a cellulosic fibrous materials is treated with a strong aqueous solutions of sodium hydroxide, the alkali resistant portion which remains un dissolved is known as α-cellulose. Upon filtration the filtrate contains dissolved material of two kinds, that portion which is precipitated when the filtrate, in neutralized is called β-cellulose where as the portion remaining in the solution is λ– cellulose progressive degradation of α-cellulose results in an increase of alkali soluble materials which appear as β- cellulose and with further de polymerization, as water soluble cellulose. Therefore, the higher the content of cellulose of the paper, the stronger it is.

(g) *Viscosity*

The viscosity of solutions of cellulose is related to the chain length or mols, wt. of the cellulose. The viscosity test is useful for detection of degradation reactions such as hydrolysis and oxidation which lead to reduced molecular weight. The higher the viscosity the long the chain length and hence the stronger is the paper.

(h) *Measurement of pH of Paper*

Because of the influence of acidity and alkalinity on the stability of paper the pH has assumed considerable importance. The pH is defined as the negative logarithm of the hydrogen ion concentration in moles per liter. As 25°C neutrality is represented by a pH of 7.0; lower values indicate increasingly acid solutions.

To measure the pH, the paper is extracted with water and the hydrogen ion concentration (pH) of the water extract is measured. The extraction can be performed with cold water on with hot water. Generally the cold extraction method gives higher pH values. Owing to hydrolysis of alum the hot water extraction gives lower values.

A method of measuring "Contact pH" is based on direct application of measuring glass electrode to the wetted paper or to a drop of water placed on the sheet. The method is quick and may serve for approximate estimation of the acidity of paper. It is non destructive and is particularly useful for examining marks of art on paper, books and documents of archival value.

(i) *Sizing, fillers, voiding and colouring*

Cellular is hydrophilic material and as such a sheet made of cellulose fire would not resist spread or penetration of water or writing ink, unless some chemicals treatment is given to prevent it. This special treatment is called "sizing" and is generally referred to as "internal" sizing in context of "surface" sizing. A sizing agent is a water resistant material which is made into an emulsion and then precipitated and fixed on the fibres by means of a salt of a multivalent metal usually aluminium sulphate, imparts paper with water resisting properties. On such paper inks or colours neither separated resisting properties. On such papers inks or colours neither spread nor penetrate the sheet in short time required by it to get dried. Resin, starch, animal glue and wax emulsion are important sizing materials in common grades of paper. Bituminous emulsion, latex and silicones are also used for special purpose Alumina is the usual precipitant which can be partly replaced by sodium aluminates and aluminum chloride.

A sheet of paper made from cellulose fibers lacks opacity and smoothness unless inside pores and unevenness of surface are filled with some fine white powder called fillers. Fillers invariably "load" or increase the mass of paper. This process is called "loading" in addition to opacity and smoothness fillers improve texture, printing quality, brightness, flatness and dimensional stability in changing atmosphere but in fiber to fiber contact. Loading of paper is accomplished by the addition of inorganic white pigments or fillers and binding adhesives. Clay is the most common white coating pigment, although calcium carbonate, titanium oxide, talc, calcium and barium sulphate are also used. The common adhesives are casein and starch. Titanium oxide is the most effective filler for improving opacity and whiteness. Calcium carbonate, zinc sulphide, and lithopone are also used as fillers for special purpose.

Paper is coloured by adding synthetic dyes or pigments. Most of the coloured paper are made by dying and the paper-maker may choose among a wide varity of dyes production of desired shade. In short, the kind of paper being made determines the requirement for non-fibrous constituent in the finished as well as for the fibrous material.

(j) Types of paper

Paper may be classified according to the raw materials from which it is made (as: rag paper, according the method of manufacture (as: handmade paper), the place of origin (as: Japanese paper) or its intended use (as: drawing paper), absorbent paper. This term includes filter paper; blotting paper and any other paper with absorbent properties. Good unsized absorbent paper is made from high-quality specially ground chemical pulp often also containing lint. Paper making Machine was invented in 1798 by Nicholas Louis. Pulp passes through two rollers which were suitably heated. Thereby the paper was dried and later rolled on a roller.

Bark cloth; sometimes known by its Hawaiian name "tapa" is a material similar to paper. It is made from the bast fibres of various members of the genus artocarpus (the bread fruit tree) and the paper mulberry (Broussonetia papyri-era) as well as of other trees. The fibres; which is some cases are first soaked and subjected to a process if fermentation are beaten into a flat structure with wooden beaten bark cloth the production of which used to be widely disseminated; is still made by the inhabitants of New guinea; the Tonga island Uganda and the area around the borders of Mexico and Guatemala. Bark cloth consists of plant fibres; as does Japanese paper but it is distinguished from paper by its method of manufacture and by its nature.

Japanese paper is handmade, very absorbent, has fibers at least 10 to 20 mm long and is sized with the sap of plants. Japanese paper is made from the bast fibers of various shrubs, particularly the paper mulberry (Broussonetia papyrifera), the gampi (wikstroemia canascens) and the mitsumata (edge-wortbia papyrifera), but it often contains softwood pulp as well. There are many varieties of Japanese paper including those that are hard, soft, fine-textured, rough, thick and thin, as well as some that are very tough and strong even when wet. A type of resistant is made from gampi and/ or mitsumata and is still sometimes used in Japan for window panes, sliding doors and umbrellas.

Papier mache is a plastic mixture of old paper, chemical pulp and fillers such as clay, gypsum with glue or starch as a binding medium, it can be coloured and pressed in moulds. Hollow formed paper machine objects are characterized by their very light weights. Dolls, figures for nativity scenes and a large variety of other objects used to be made from paper machine.

Parchment paper (also known a grease proof paper) is made by dipping un sized paper that contains no fillers into sulphuric acid for a short time then neutralizing and rinsing it. The sulphuric acid causes the cellulose in the paper to swell to a jelly-like consistency and to be converted to hydrocellulose which shrinks to a close-textured skin when it dries. Parchment paper is very tough, translucent and water-resistant in contrast to ordinary paper it is impervious to fats and oils.

Plate paper used for etchings and engravings must be soft, must handle well and must be absorbent so that when dampened, it can be pressed in to the grooves in the plate in order to take up the printer's ink effectively. Today soft paper made from chemical pulp with or without some rag content so used for intaglio printing. plate paper is unsized and not located .

Rag paper was produced in Europe before the 19th century was made from rags and other textile scraps and from re-used plant fiber products such as rope and nets. Today rag paper is made in small quantities from linters and textile scraps for special purposes only such as bank notes, intaglio printing, very expensive writing paper, etc.

Rosin-sized paper and board machine – made paper produced since the 19th century has generally had rosins and aluminium sulphate added to the pulp as a size: because of the low pH, this paper is less durable than earlier paper that was surface – sized with gelatin or starch. Rosin – sized board and paper, that is those containing aluminum sulphate, should be avoided when restoring, or making mounts for, prints and drawings; also in the restoration of books.

(k) Tissue Paper

Tissue is a general term covering various very thin types of paper whose weight is less than $25g/m^2$ – Japanese tissues weighs only 6 to 8 g/m^2. Tissue paper made with long fibres of flax, etc. is comparatively strong.

11. LEATHER BINDING

Animal skin which has been cured and tanned is called 'Leather'. Usually leather from large animals like cattle, horses other big animal is known as hide and that from smaller animals like pig, calf, goat, sheep etc. is called as skin. The skin of an animal consists of an outer layer epidermis, the middle layer is called corium or dermis and the inner layer is called hypodermis, within the corium there exists two more layers namely the papillary layer in which the hair follicles are situated and the reticular layer which consists of a dense network of randomly oriented convective tissue fiber intersperses with blood vessels. The reticular layer determines the tensile strength of the leather. The hide from a freshly flayed animal contains about 33% protein. Mineral constituents, fat, carbohydrate account for the remaining. Almost 70-90% of the total protein constitutes of collagen and the rest is composed of protein elastin. It is the corium layer which is used to make the leather book binding. Various treatments are given to the skin before it is tanned. The tanned skin, the epidermis together with the hair and the hypodermis are removed. The skin is first subjected to sweating or liming where the hair, epidermis and flesh are loosened which is then removed. The epidermis and hair are then scraped off . This is followed by splitting and deliming .

To transform a skin into leather, tanning is done. For this tanning agents are used which crosslink the collagen molecule and form a stable fibrous lattice. This renders the proteins immune to putrification and prevent their swelling in cold water and transforming into gelatin in boiling water. Various methods can be followed for tanning leather such as vegetable tanning using tannins from the bark and leaves of certain species of a trees, alum tanning using aluminium, potassium sulphate solution, chromium salts, zirconium salts, formaldehyde and so on. The tanned leather is then lubricated using various oils and fats like tallow, neat's foot oil, fish oil etc.

Leather for Book Binding was formerly made from the entire skin. However in later periods it was being made from the Flesh side of the split skin. The whole skin is limed, de haired and de fleshed. The splitting machine separates the skin from the flesh side. It is put on a frame and scraped from both sides with a crescent shaped knife. It is thus dried under stretched condition. It is washed with hot water and then rubbed with a pumice block. Alkalinity protects parchment from the attack of the biological agencies since they prefer a substratum of slightly acid in character. It is also stable against acid pollutants and is, therefore, more durable than leather.

Disadvantage of alkalinity is yellowing of the parchment. It is necessary to understand the nature of leather and parchment and the fact as to why they need processing.

Both chemically and structurally these materials are complex which involve the interaction of many types of tissues that these are made, consisting of innumerable bundles of protein fibers- collagen. These molecules are long and are naturally oriented during their formation into fibers and their bundles. These are by its nature are interweaved in a three dimensional manner through the thickness of the skin, but the structure is not homogenous. Many leather scrolls are extant from the periods c.1300-1100 BC.

Chapter Three

FACTORS OF DETERIORATION

Though primarily the self life of a manuscript is dependent on the quality of paper and other materials used and binding materials that might have been used in it's making, yet it has been observed that due to poor quality materials, binding technique or improper or rough usage much physical damage and harm results. This, if not corrected well in time, may lead to irrepairable loss. In the manuscript reposetries, it is very common to come across manuscripts where a few sections in the beginning or end have loosened from the spine with the result that the sheets or leaves either sag within the cover, if any or get separated and become loose from the cover.

Seperation of leaves, tears at the fore edge, and their crumbling; crockling of leather, tears in the binding cloth at the spine and the corners etc. are some of the damages in the binding and become noticeable at an early stage. Sometimes drawings and illustrations get separated from the text, if these materials are not properly inserted or bound at the respective places and fixed tightly or firmly they get mixed up and eventually are lost. It is also not uncommon to see manuscripts where sheets get stuck up into a solid mass due to being stored in repeatedly humid and dry climatic cycles. Care in separation of such blocked sheets is also necessary so that the pages could be opened without any damage. Besides the above physical damages, fluffy blackish or greyish growth of mildew on the leather cover and cloth also gradually eat away these materials leaving stains. The growth of these micro-organisms also attracts other biological pests like psocids which results in further damage.

Before we venture the factors of decay of various types of manuscripts it is better to know the impact of various factors in detail. Staining of it increases by damp, dust, dirt and presence of iron particulate matter. It is hygroscopic and can absorb in any amount of moisture. Hydrolysis results into complete breakdown of the structure with ultimate formation of gelatin or the parchment size. It swells and shrinks with the increase and decrease of RH. It is subjected to fungus attack only. The leather manuscripts are best preserved in extremely dry conditions and in anaerobic environment.

(1)Natural Factors concerning Environment. (2)Manmade Factors. (3)Biological Factors (4) Ignorance factors (5)Inherent Factors (6)Chemical Factors (7)Physical/Mechanical Factors.

NATURAL FACTORS

Environmental factors include humidity, temperature, light and pollution. The temperature and RH through out the year is recommended by experts (Garry Thomson and others) to be 55% to 60% and temperature between 18 to 22 degrees Celsius, with a provision of air filters of at least 60% efficiency and activated carbon filters to check acid producing pollutant gases not to exceed $10mg/mm^3$. Most of the materials of the manuscripts are hygroscopic and have vacant spaces in between their cellular structure which varies according to it's very nature. This vacant space has a capacity to attract and store water vapor from the environment and looses it till it has come in equilibrium with the RH vapor of it's surroundings.

It is a fact that the moisture content of the object adjusts itself accordingly. But the decay is more in those circumstances when these parameters are changing very frequently and are rapid, sometimes high and at times very low. Fibers of plant materials absorb moisture and swell when conditions become humid and shrink when there are dry conditions. This is basically due to the change in the moisture content of the document and is proportional to the RH of the surrounding environment. This phenomenon of swelling and shrinking can be adjusted by the fibers when fresh and in good state of preservation but they cannot adjust itself accordingly when they become old with age. Documentary heritage is Organic in composition and mostly it constitutes of Plant materials. They become limp or get stiff and brittle very frequently in the tropical and sub-tropical conditions. This makes them easily prone to damage if kept in a wrong storage and is subjected to frequent handling or at times mishandling. If found in bound volumes the individual leaves may get physical contact with the adjoining leaf accidently with high moisture content or water due to seepage from the roof /leaking drain pipes resulting into wetting or free contact with water especially in the event of floods and fire which may be extinguished with aqueous methods through water hydrants instead of gaseous fire extinguishers. This would make the leaves stuck to each other in pairs or as a whole. There are many ways of extinguishing fire by cutting the oxygen levels nearby. Water would extinguish fire but also damage the documentary heritage for ever.

This is true about Leather book bindings as the fat content in the leather increases, it's water resistance and tensile strength may also increase. Natural voids in the leather or those resulting from chemical modifications need oils and fat thus increasing the support an solidity of the leather. Time sets that we should plan for controlling the environmental conditions which need to be kept under check neither too high nor too low since both these conditions degrade the documentary heritage. These parameters have to vary according to the geographical location of the heritage. The ideal RH is 50% and 65%, the temperature at 18-20 degrees Celsius. Absorption of light will not directly cleave a bond in the cellulose chain. However certain additives, impurities, dyes and metals such as iron (Fe++, Fe+++) will absorb energy from light which rises their electrons to a higher energy orbit. When this energy is released to the cellulose, bond cleavage can result and this, in turn can allow oxidation degradation of cellulose.

Oxidation degradation is found when oxygen is absorbed at certain sites on cellulose molecule. With oxygen absorption we will find an increase in oxygen containing groups such as Carboxylic acids. As this greatly increases level of acid is released the cellulose will be hydrolyzed (meaning the covalent between the rings in the cellulose chain will be broken forming two shorter chains and releasing a hydrogen ion). Oxidation will also cause colour changes. Similarly light intensity for documentary heritage should be 50 lux and the intake of pollution level should be restricted to minimum by proper circulation of air. Especially the acidic and alkaline fumes from outdoor or indoor sources to be kept under check. Pollutant gases like sulphur di oxide (26 micro grams per cubic meter), carbon di oxide (120 micrograms per cubic meter), sulphur trioxide (3micrograms per cubic meter), ammonia (60 micrograms per cubic meter), hydrochloric acid (15 micrograms per cubic meter), hydrofluoric acid (2 micrograms per cubic meter) and hydrogen sulphide (28 micrograms per cubic meter). Pollution is another source of degradation of indoor materials in Libraries, Archives, Museums and other historic buildings. Dust, soot, residues of tobacco smoke, alkaline aerosols are all encountered in the soiling of manuscripts and other documents including historic artifacts and the last but not the least the visitors and staff. Two terms are in common use for the solid particles suspended in the air particulates and aerosol. The former is used here as particulates that settle in still air can be termed as dust. They vary largely in size from 1000 microns to a hundredth of a micron in diameter. The particulates arise largely from the burning of fuels in power station and are emitted by vehicles and from the heating systems there is a lot of sooty and tarry material in them, which can work as a catalysts and start the deterioration. Though the primary effect of particulate deposition is a loss of visual quality (aesthetic) that may affect some of the materials into abrasion, and scratching.

MANMADE FACTORS

Another source of pollutants are the formaldehyde resins used in the manufacture of plywood, particle board, other material of indoor structures of wood, other material used for partition walls and storage cupboards. Rubber, Bakelite, Plasticine and some plastics are dangerous for museum and library holdings or display cases with lead pigmented paints or effluents emitted by the vehicles near major roads and other furnishings containing sulphur which is present in materials like ply wood and boards.

It is recognized that the only effective protection for collections as a whole is full, ducted air conditioning with filtration to remove particulate matter of macro and micro levels. However, the effectiveness of such systems is greatly reduced if they are not properly designed and maintained. Measures to control pollutants brought by the visitors, if not followed strictly may bring the pollutants while entering the display areas. Manuscripts become brittle and discolour quickly with the rise in temperature and humidity. The action is thus two fold one the decay of the composition and the second the fading of light sensitive materials.

I remember a man made lapse, 30 years back while I was Head of the conservation department of the National Museum and Late Dr. N.R. Banerjee was the then Director NM, telephoned me to see him at once to look into this unprecedent problem in the first floor gallery where the Central Asian Antiquities were displayed. It was reported to him that some showcases in the above mentioned gallery, are experiencing some vibrations in the floor from the roof of the ground floor. I examined the problem and found that the ducting in this gallery does not have any shock absorbing material .This was brought to the notice of the CPWD responsible for maintenance of the building and I along with the Director had an urgent meeting with them to rectify the problem.

It is a fact that manuscripts have suffered in India because of many adverse reasons such as proper management of the collections, lack of proper buildings, inadequate funds, unscientific attitude leading to improper approach to the problems facing such institutions and lack of trained staff. The situation thus became very bad due to the wrong storage conditions, inadequate and improper maintenance. This is due to lack of understanding of the use of faulty materials, because of the mismanagement of the Libraries and manuscript collections in the past in the various shrines and *Mathas* This was the basic reasons of the fact that we do not find many surviving examples of our vast documentary heritage which we very often hear about them and collected over the bygone centuries. Only those collections could survive which had some sort of maintenance and others were lost with time. That is why our ancient documentary heritage was lost for posterity. This type of attempts to keep the manuscript in bundles and tightly tying them exerts pressure on the fragile leaves breaking them into pieces. In view of the unscientific repairs by adhesive or tapes and cello-tape, repair by rapidly decaying materials and adhesives like animal glue only add to the problems especially when some areas a great tendency to deteriorate as early as than the papers made up from long fibers. The short fibers do not have that much tendency to retain the loadings or sizing materials for a long period and hence such type of fibers are attacked very early covered by such tapes which hide the text increase the problems for the restorer who are asked to conserve them now.

I have witnessed a case when an illustrated manuscript leaf was covered from the back side with a thick paper using glue even though it had even the text at the reverse side. Such bad repairs proving the illustration was having a text at the back or front proving its authenticity only add to the problems instead of solving them scientifically. Bad restoration as stated above is no restoration/conservation. In case of palm leaves and Sanchi pat manuscripts usually a hole is made for allowing the hard cord to pass through them which due to friction, has a chance to get bigger and bigger with the lapse of time almost in all leaves. Use of poor quality material contaminates whether for repair, display cases or storing them in boxes which are acidic themselves will only add to the acid content thus adding to more decay.

As a matter of fact most of the archives, museums and manuscript collections (*Granthagars*) in our country did not have a properly planned building which should have provision of a planned storage, protection against fire, flood and other natural disasters resulting into calamities and improper ventilation for the circulation of air. With the development and creation of many industries in India, indoor pollutants in libraries, museums and historic houses originate for the most part from out gassing of structural or decorative materials, heating plants or heaters, the activities of visitors and staff, and by the intrusion of outdoor pollutants. In special cases the artifacts themselves may emit significant gases and even dangerous amounts of polluting gases. Paper and similar writing materials suffer due to sulphur di oxides in making it fragile and discolored in conjunction of moisture, physical wear and tear and acidic materials introduced at the time of manufacture process. This results in decreased folding endurance, pH change, molecular weight measurement and tensile strength. Attention to indoor air quality standards for cultural property specially the manuscripts has been directed to the intrusive pollutants like sulphur di oxide, nitrous oxide and particulate matters. There is enough evidence that indoor air pollution causes significant damage to photographs, paper, leather and dyes demonstrating effects of immediate consequence.

BIOLOGICAL FACTORS

I often say that what the environment could not do in centuries the biological growth can do overnight and is, therefore, most dangerous for the library and manuscript repositories whether it is natural or accidental.

(a) Micro_organisms

I have witnessed damages growing over night or slowly. Spores of micro-organisms are present in the environment and remain in the dormant stage but get activated as soon as they get favourable conditions to multiply very quickly. General mould growth occurs, almost invariably, when the relative humidity rises to a level within the growing range of fungi. When kept in a hot dry atmosphere the leaves become crisp, brittle and dehydrated. When the conditions become humid the growth of various micro-organisms obscured by mould "bloom" could change the look of the text and illustration. A light growth almost bloom of mould, will often occur in one area of the library where the ventilation is poor, and in some libraries, where conditions are even static, this faint bloom may not increase during long periods. It may not occur when the air control plant fails without breakdown of AC being detected. Local spots on a book, drawing, itching, water colour print and many other paper materials get these spots due to hygroscopic nature of the cover, moisture trapped in between, local high RH in a small space or the paper material coming in contact with wet surroundings due to floods on several books staged together and even a book remained isolated & neglected for a long period will grow general thick moulds.

General Foxing fungus may appear as brown spots of fungus and black spots on paper products in isolated spots as fungal growth. The yellow to reddish brown stains often left on paper may appear as micro-organisms which are known as foxing marks. The colour most probability is due to the organic waste products left by them. In addition, ferruginous impurities in paper leave rust like stains specially when the RH is high. Foxing can be distinguished from iron spots under UV irradiations which cause foxing to fluoresce where as the iron marks would appear black.

The following species of fungi grow on palm leaf, sanchi pat, leather and paper etc. whenever their growing conditions are suitable for their growth. Dirty environment, unhigenic stagnant surroundings and no body to disturb them promote their growth. This is a law of nature to become many from the one. Our Vedic texts refer to this phenominun as, "*Eko aham bahusyami*".

(1) Aspergillus niger (2) Aspergillus glaucus (3) Aspergillus flavus (4) Aspergillus restricus (5) Aspergillus ochraceous (6) Penicillium sp. and many more in our subtropical conditions..

(b) Insects

Insects are equally devastating for library and manuscript collections of Palm leaves, Sanchi pat, and Paper including their leather bindings or card board cover with-textile cover in tropical climatic conditions with the exception of birch bark due to some natural inclusions in it's structure which are insect repellents. Damage to manuscripts by insects is very characteristic and can indicate the presence of insects which damage them. The insects which damage the books, manuscripts bound or unbound are four types namely, Silverfish (Lepisma saccharina), Cockroaches (Blattella orientalis) which are regarded as household pests in India, subterranean Termites and Indian bookworm Beetle (Gastrallus indicus).

The Silver fish slightly etches the surface of paper and other library products making irregular patterns, Surface of paper and other library materials particularly the binding is roughened by Cockroaches on the other hand by chewing, the roughness having been caused by pulling action by them. Feces pliers of some of the species as large as those of a mouse. Feces deposits often leave dark smears or stains. Indian book worm beetle (Gastrallus indicus) leaves on books with it's binding circular pin holes about 1mm in diameter. Such holes are found inside the binding and through the pages parallel sided tunnels, of about 1-1.5mm width while it feeds on their materials of filled with irregular feces pellets etc. Damage is more prominent towards the sides and less in the middle of the book. Similar type of damage is found on palm leaf manuscripts and Sanchi pat manuscripts including their cover whether of leather or card board.

During my visits to several parts of India, Indonesia a large number of palm leaf manuscripts and paper manuscripts besides printed books have also been damaged by book worms and book lice making them almost unusable unless restored properly. There have been some cases of such damaged manuscripts having been submerged in water by putting them in rivers (*Jal Prabah*) for religious reasons and rituals. During my visit to Mathura it was confirmed by *Priests* of some temples and *Mattas*. Damaged statues and manuscripts are not kept in the temples for worship. They make circular holes inside the binding and through the pages are found parallel sided tunnels, filled with irregular ball like materials. Damage is more towards the sides and less in the middle of the book. Spine of the binding is most affected. Termites make holes on book bindings including leather binding, palm leaf, Sanchi pat and paper lined with excreta and earth cemented together. Tunnels are irregular when on books and manuscripts well struck mastic like frass. All these would make these materials weak, fragile and delicate besides disfiguring them and often pages are stuck to each other.

As regards leather bindings are concerned, moisture content between 12% to 14% keeps it's fiber flexible but if the moisture content decreases below the above mentioned limits, they become stiff and brittle. High moisture content on the other hand promotes fungus/mould growth on the surface of the bindings and high temperature above 50 degree cent. may lead to irreversible shrinkage and hardening. Light bleaches both dyed leather and pigmented finished leather. Acid and alkaline residues from the manufacturing processes make leather brittle and very intense sweating or liming causes damage to the skins or hides even before they are tanned. A serious form of damage results into breakage of fibers and finally making them powdery which turns into brick –red colour (red rot). The main cause of red –rot is sulphur–dioxide which forms sulphuric acid in the leather. Since it is a strong acid the pH goes very high and has a destructive action on the grains of the book binding. Other pollutant gases like nitrogen oxide contributes in its degradation affecting leather directly and attacking the peptide linkages in the collagen molecules. oxidation and hydrolytic breakdown further.

IGNORANCE FACTORS

Most of the collections did not have the provision of periodic inspection of the stores so that one knows what is going on in the stores to take timely action before it is too late. We should not have any chance of managerial apathy and if I may say so accountability for the wrong attitude in case of our cultural heritage. The display cases may be of three types. (a) Air tight,(b)Free flow of air from the gallery to the inside of the cases and (c) Air is allowed through a small holes with dust filter. The exhibition area may be controlled or uncontrolled. Controlled environment may be achieved by the following:-

(1) For the whole building ie. Central Air Conditioning unit.

(2) For the Exhibition area/room.ie. Packaged Air conditioning unit.

(3 For the Individual Show case i.e. Closed cases with buffers taking care of dust, pollutant gases.

(i) Air conditioning should be with Filters, (a) Rough filters, (b) High efficiency Filters. (c) Activated Carbon filters.

(4) We can have Airtight Cases in a Controlled environment.

(i) We should try that dust and pollutants are minimized including the micro dust.

(ii) There should be arrangements for the temperature and RH control.

All exhibits displayed should be kept at the gallery temperature and RH before displaying them in air tight cases. The constructional materials such as wood, ply board, fiber board, cloth etc. should be conditioned for 2-3 weeks prior to their use for making showcases or the open showcase may be kept in the controlled gallery before the objects i.e. manuscripts are displayed in them. This should stabilize the equilibrium of the moisture content of all exhibits displayed.

INHERANT FACTORS

Inherent factors such as composition, source and method of making or manufacture also play an important part in the deterioration of these manuscripts. The deterioration of paper is dependent on its original raw material because some papers are made from having very short fibrous raw material which have a great tendency to deteriorate as early as than the papers made from long fibers. The short fibers do not have that much tendency to retain the loadings or sizing materials for a long period and hence such type of fibers are attacked very early by the humidity and light etc. to get deteriorated. The long fiberous material mostly used for the durable paper due to it they have a bearing tendency of loading and sizing materials. Such type of paper is having tendency to resist humidity and light. Although the cellulose will be the water absorbent substance the long fibers do not loose their moisture content as early as possible like short fibers. The water retention value is always more in long fibers than that of shorter ones. The pulping processes is also important to count the internal causes for deterioration of paper, because some pulping are carried out by chemical method and some by mechanical method. The pulp made by chemical process carries very good strength whereas the pulp done by mechanical process produce very weak and short fibers; such type of fibers neither have tendency to bear more weight nor resists from light or humidity so it starts to decay in the resistance favourable condition.

The short fiberous paper chemically react very easily with the atmospheric elements. The oxidation reaction takes place with the chemicals in paper and the cellulosic fibers start to become brittle. More inferior is the paper more it is susceptible to decay. News paper for instance yellows in a very short time. All rag paper is most durable and thus long lasting as it is all cellulose. Lignin on the other hand, in them gets oxidized with photo chemical action of light and the long polymer chain breaks resulting into depolymerization and loosening of strength. This also results into yellowing of fibers and at times results into dis-colouration of them.

Carbon Black Ink contains only carbon in resins and is reported to have been used from very early times. Indian Ink is also reported to be produced by grinding of carbon black particles in water and gum or glue. It is soluble. However, if it has to be water proof it is mixed with Shellac and borax. The use of acidic inks like the Iron Gall ink which is a combination of tannic, gallic and dilute hydrochloric acid with an iron salt, phenol and a blue or black dye. which was started in the 12th cent. A.D.. However, if exposed to day light continuously these would fade or colour change could happen besides being acidic in character it eats away. The original writing would be blue but it would change to black since ferric tannate is produced changing ferrous to ferric. The paper or acidic pigments like Basic Copper Acetate and iron gall ink can attack the cellulose to char the paper or decays and make perforations which make it very weak and fragile. Residual acidity and alkalinity can also come with time.

We also notice that the individual pages may stick with each other especially in the bound volumes or even otherwise if there is little pressure in between them because of the size which becomes loose or dissolves whenever the relative humidity is high. With age the size gets weaker and weaker day by day and the paper bcomes very weak loosing the size due to increased RH and becomes very fragile, brittle loosing it's flexibility and elasticity. The sizing material is also food for micro-organisms and insects. Neglect accelerates the decay. There are missing pages, bands and head bands, covers and corners are broken. Loosening of the pages due to damage of the spine if the old stitches have broken which often is the case. Palm leaf, Birch bark, Sanchi pat all plant materials contain high lignin and natural adhesives which loose there adhesive properties over the period.

On the other hand paper which came much later has been sized and at times loaded to make it suitable for writing and smooth to improve the look. for this purpose it has been bleached using acidic chemicals and additives have been added to make it more white and smooth. It also absorbs polluting gases such as sulphur di oxide and nitrogen containing gases to change it's acidity content and deteriorates the paper thus reducing it's life.

CHEMICAL FACTORS

The third mechanism of decay results from the photo chemical degradation of polymers in short chain molecules into de polymerisation triggering off photolysis. At the same time the activated oxygen can react with water leading to the formation of hydrogen per oxide having a reducing action on the colours of the binding. Acidity might often develop in the stored leaves from the continual exchange between atmospheric moisture and the materials such as adhesives and vegetable tanned leather in the binding and particularly the spine area. Traces of specific metals such as copper, iron and manganese might remain in them to act as catalysts to convert sulphur dioxide absorbed by the leather into sulphuric acid and may promote further decay of the constituent materials.

Iron tannate inks also cause problem of acidity in the manuscripts. As with the leather, environmental condition as discussed above can accelerate chemical decay in the form of discolorations, which appear earlier on the spine than on boards and are caused mainly by harmful radiations of the light. Rodents such as rats destruct the books and manuscripts into small pieces to eat as food.

Chemical staining e.g. rusting, discolouration, photo chemical action of light resulting into de-polymerization of the cellulose, oxidation of the lignin and changes in the colour tones besides yellowing of organic plant materials. Intensity of light above 75 microwatt is harmful and need to be controlled while manuscripts are on display and UV radiation up to 25lux will minimize the damage. Both intensity and duration of exposure are very crucial because these are most active with the rise of humidity and temperature both for chemical reaction to start solubility of the ink and colours also depends on the medium's solubility. It is also reported that the natural adhesive which keeps the layers together, some chemicals may dislodge them resulting into further separation of the layers. Chemical may decay the support itself and make them fragile and brittle due to degradation of lignin by oxidation.

Photo chemical action is due to the UV rays and the radiation in this range of near UV and in first three radiations of the spectrum i.e. violet, indigo and blue of the vibgyor. That is perhaps the indigenous reason of wrapping the manuscripts in red cotton cloth. The original size with age gets weaker if subjected to aqueous treatment for cleaning or de-acidification to weaken it further making it very fragile and brittle loosing it's elasticity and flexibility.

Permanance of paper- It also depends on low percentage of filling material (loading) and sizing. Following specifications for paper permanence have been prescribed by ISI(IS 1774-1980).

(1)	Rag content	100%
(2)	Alpha Cellulose	85%
(3)	Copper number	2 maximum
(4)	Ash content	2 maximum
(5)	Rosin content	1.5 maximum
(6)	pH	5.5 minimum

Papers become acidic due to polluted atmosphere, acid inducing iron or copper particles imbedded in fibres from manufacture; residues of bleaches, impurities, acid sizing like alum hardened gelatin and alum-rosin sizing; acidic pigments and inks like iron gall ink. Acidity in paper is one of the principal reasons for it's decay. Acidity causes loss of strength by hydrolysis of the cellulose molecule, a reaction eventually break up their long chain polymeric structure into unstable fractions. The acidic pollution consists mainly of sulphur dioxide and sulfuric acid, while ozone is the most damaging oxidant pollutant is ozone. Natural gases produce SO_2 which is further oxidized into SO_3 which in conjunction with moisture would form sulfuric acid. Nitrous acid further is converted into Nitric acid. It is a strong acid which hydrolyzes the cellulose.

PHYSICAL/MECHANICAL FACTORS

Constant use of manuscript is the need of their very presence in a museum and the manuscript collections for their study by scholars and museum professionals. We should, therefore, set norms which have to be observed by one and all in interest of heritage. Creases and folds have to be checked not to happen. Dust, dirt and soiling to be vacuum cleaned before they become unmanageable.

Tears, cracks are not allowed to increase further. One of the causes of physio-mechanical damage in leather book bindings is due to frequent fluctuations of relative humidity and we should manage their moisture content so that it is, neither low nor high, so as to keep them flexible and are not allowed to become brittle which may result into cracking .This may result into grain separation from the fiber network layer. Desiccation due to abrupt swelling and shrinking may result into a process that becomes irreversible in old leather bindings. During the 16th century alum-tawed bookbinding leather is coated with an albumen layer. This albumen layer, usually identifiable by the smooth, shiny surface usually hardened the grain causing cracks. Physico-mechanical damage to leather may also be due to earlier conservation treatments, which have disturbed the leather's natural water balance.

We should use cotton gloves and ink pens should not be allowed in the storage, instead pencils should be used for taking notes when scholars are examining them. Scholars have to be told to observe the rules which are related to their long time preservation. Proper awareness of safety measures should be followed sooner the better. In the past not many of these precautions have been adhered to. Since we can not take large samples from the manuscripts and documents as is the case in many Laboratories such as the Geological Survey Of India or Archaeological survey of India etc, in the case of museums and libraries our National Laboratories can be contacted to take very small samples from unimportant places and use instrumental analysis and help in the diagnosis of the exact problem.

(i) Instrumental Analysis

The under mentioned instruments which are available in the Laboratory of the National archives of India, New Delhi and the National research laboratory for Conservation of Cultural Property, Lucknow can be of help in deciding the future course of action.

1. Microscopy at medium magnification, 2. Photography in visible and invisible radiations. 3. pH meter. 4. Colour measurement. 5. Conductivity meter. 6. Folding strength, 7. Tensile strength, 8. Brusting strength, 9. Tear strength, 10. Accelerated ageing tests, 11. Steriomicroscope, 12. Pollution monitoring equipment, 13. Porosimeter, 14. SEM, and 15. Moisture meter.

Cellulose is a hygroscopic material, naturally white, neutral to organic solvents and long chain polymeric compound. There are different kinds of Cellulose like, hemicelluloses, alpha, beta and gamma cellulose. However alpha is an important one among all celluloses which can be found more generally in paper and cotton. Cellulose is having traces of mannose and xylose residues and on hydrolysis give glucose which is a degradadative compound. As compared to the paper, birch bark is more resistant to water, liquid, insect and microbial attack. It absorbs no water or any liquid.

According to a study cited in bibliography results of Physical properties estimated in a sample are as follows which can give the picture about a sample as under.

	Before Ageing	After Ageing		
Wt or grammage, gms/m^2	47.37	24	48	72hrs.
Thickness microns	37.2	-	-	-
Density grms/cm^3	05.1	-	-	-
Tensile index N. m/g	16.2	16.0	15.8	15.1
Stretch	0.4	0.3	0.3	0.2
Folds at 0.5kg	721	701	556	418
Brusting index kpa m^2/g	3.93	3.8	2.24	1.04
Tear index m N.m^2/g	4.56	3.82	3.15	2.48

(ii) Simple tests for Analysis of Materials

Rosin has been used in the sizing of paper for example has a deleterious effect on its life. It, therefore, may help in taking care of it to test for presence/ absence. Concentrated solution of sugar and a drop of H_2SO_4 gives red colour on the edge of the drop.

Any paper which contains Exparto grass can not be of age prior to 1861 AD any paper sample which contains chemical wood pulp can not be of age prior to 1880 A.D. any paper which contains mechanical wood pulp can not be of prior to 1885 AD. Dating of paper can be done on the basis, that iron gall ink was first in the 12th cent. AD where as Indian ink and carbon ink were being used earlier than that. Analysis of paper and other conventional writing materials to indicate the nature of the products has to be made clear.

Reaction with Herbeg's Stains	
Pure Cellulose (Cotton, Linen)	Wine Red
Lignified Cellulose (Wood, Grass etc.)	Yellow or Yellow changing Slowly to Blue.
Purified Cellulose (Chemical wood Pulp)	Blue, grey or Voilet.

This matter has been dealt in detail by me in my book Aspects of Heritage Study (2004) cited in the Bibliography.

Chapter Four

STEPS IN CONSERVATION AND RESTORATION OF MANUSCRIPTS

1. SEGRIGATION

Segrigation of manuscripts which are in good condition from those which are in decaying condition is the first step. Only those manuscripts which are in good condition can be preserved by Digitization while others have to wait till they are conserved scientifically so as to make them stand even the very little physical force.

Having understood the chemical composition of the various materials used in them, method of making of the manuscripts and having acquainted with the forces of their decay, the next step is to chalk out a policy to be adopted for their Preventive and Curative Conservation and restoration as per the latest thinking of all the involved measures, techniques and scientific interest by distinguished scientists in ancient materials that a beginning about the study of components and fabrication of materials should be initiated. Study of the technology of making art objects which has a strong bearing on their conservation, a beginning of scientific conservation started in India after the Independence, which could be used for keeping them in good state of Preservation for posterity. All damaged or insect affected manuscripts should immediately be separated from the manuscripts which are still in good shape as the artists made them initially. This safety measure will stop the infection to spread further in the entire collection. The target is to kill the micro-organisms and their spores or the insects and their dormant eggs. Gaseous Fumigation is a sure method for this purpose but selection of fumigant is a very important step as it should not be harmful for the manuscripts as well as for it's contents. Various general steps in their conservation /restoration are as follows.

Many institutions having manuscript, do not visit their collections periodically and, therefore, they know about the infection when the insects are visible coming out from the storage area and when the insects have done the damage. As stated above the first thing to do is to segregate other manuscripts which are still in good condition. Some institutions are very vigilant while others lack the smartness so as to fumigate their manuscripts as soon as acquisition in their collection at the time of their entry. This would save the rest of the collection since the infection detected, has to be killed. Some are resorting to fumigation as a periodic exercise to keep them away. All insect damaged manuscripts were fumigated by various techniques already approved by the Head of the laboratory. Various chemicals are being used for fumigation and should not be used for reasons of toxicity as these may be harmful for the operators as well as for the different constituents of the manuscript.

Active infection of manuscript, if visible, the first thing to do is to, segregate other manuscripts as stated above, which are still in a good condition. Microbiological infection due to spores or active eggs of the insects are the quick source of spreading the infection very quickly under favorable condition for the activity to grow fast. Some institutions are fumigating their manuscripts at that point in time i.e. before mixing them into a collection to control the infection under check not to infect the objects in good condition at the time of entry in an institution. This would save their collection since the infection detected has been killed. Some are resorting to fumigation as periodic exercise.

2. EXAMINATION AND DOCUMENTATION

The visual and close examination is conducted of the various components of the manuscript and the finding are noted to get acquainted with the decay so as to chalk out a scheme for conducting the minimum required conservation. For this purpose various instrumental and chemical tests are performed as described in above chapters. In the past conservators did not keep the detailed record of their condition which has been neglected perhaps due to the priorities of museums e.g. exhibitions in house or being sent abroad for exhibitions in other countries. In early fifties we had a very busy time especially, I have seen the National museum exhibitions being mounted in the various halls, later in seventies and eighties the entire laboratory was busy making the manuscripts suitable for display or storage and in making condition reports of the exhibits being sent abroad. The laboratory officers and staff were also deputed to examine their suitability to travel to countries near as well as very far.

3. PREPARATION OF CONDITION REPORT

The next step is the. preparation of the Condition Report and the scientific investigations conducted to come to definite conclusion and keeping the findings for the information of the conservator who would need them in future to undertake any treatment to the manuscripts and also evaluate the usefulness of the treatment conducted in the past so as to take necessary action in future. A formulated scheme for documenting their condition is appended in this book.

4. FUMIGATION

Chemicals such as Thymol (Isopropyl-meta-cresol $C_{10}H_{14}O$) is being used by many Conservators all over the country even now. I myself have used this for years together since it is low toxic when I was still in service.

Thymol fumigation is effective when 20-120g is used in a m3 size fumigation chamber which is sealed and has a inbuilt heating arrangement at the base so that it can be converted into gaseous phase to reach every nick and corner of the chamber. It is most effective in a vacuum operated chamber as the entire (*pothi* or *puthi*) book can be made air free whose place is taken by the fumigant thymol. Some workers have warned not to use it if it affects the ink and pigments. This aspect has to be studied before it's use. Baynes Cope has reported that this process may change the colour of the manuscript which would be difficult to restore back . So it should not be used if it changes the look as well as the ink. Many other fumigants such as 5% Ortho-phenyl phenol can be used safely in case of insect infection in the form of insecticidal paper which can be used to wrap such manuscripts as it can be used as a repellent for insects. Para di chloro benzene has also been used in India very frequently by many institutions which is effective in taking care of fungus and insects both.

Formaldehide is reported to have been used for mass disinfection of documents and archival heritage to eliminate danger of widespread potentials of mass-disinfection and control of insects. During my visit, I remember that once the Library of the NRLC Lucknow was being disinfected a few years back using this chemical.40% aqueous solution of formaldehyde in water was used for the purpose successfully. Many chemicals such as Ethylene oxide which is a toxic gas and which has to be used as a mixture with carbonic oxide (9:1) using vacuum chamber to eliminate the fungus infection. Many institutions in India such as the National Archives of India, New Delhi and the National Library at Kolkata both have a Vacuum fumigation Chamber for disinfecting the books and other documents in their collection on a large scale. The chamber has temperature and vacuum recorder fitted in it. The fumigant consist of ethylene oxide and carbon di oxide (C_2 S_4 O and CO_2) mixture in the ratio stated above by weight. Ethylene oxide gas is liquid at ordinary temperature under high pressure. The cylinder containing the mixture is connected to the chamber through a volatilizer. In between the two, there is a solenoid valve to prevent excess gas into the chamber. The books are kept in fan wise condition into the chamber on wire net steel trolley. The pressure is reduced to 2-3 inches inside the chamber. As soon as this vacuum is created, the valves are tightened, so as not to allow entry of the air. Ethoxide gas in cylinder is shaken and released from the cylinder. It passes through the volatilizer kept at about 65-70 degrees centigrade. Heated gas has a temperature of about 31 degrees centigrade. At the end of suitable exposure time, the vacuum is released and the air inlet valve is opened. As soon as the vacuum comes down just before reaching effusion point, the air intake valve is closed. The blower is switched on and run for about 15-20 minutes for evacuating the dilute residual gas from the chamber.

Conservators in US, Ballard and Baer in 1984 have brought the attention of conservators about the risks involved in the operation of this system not only for the Operators but even otherwise cited in the detailed paper mentioned in the bibliography. They have reported that the use of Ethylene oxide as a fumigant in museums, libraries and archives presents an excellent case for risk assessment and risk management. Both men and materials are exposed and we are to clear some questions which require answers before a proper risk management strategy should be developed to ensure harm full effects to the human and the cultural materials. We in India should conduct further research in this case so that we come to some conclusions in view of this technique being used in two major institutions of India as stated above.

On the other hand Methyl bromide and Ethylene oxide liquid have also been used in the recent past separately but in liquid phase by many institutions elsewhere for micro-biological control specially in Japan. Besides these measures the current discussion among the conservators is the Insect Pest Management (IPM) which includes the study /management of insect and micro-organism activities. This includes the study and control of the environmental conditions in the building housing the documentary heritage so that we know what to do and when. In other words the attempt is to reduce the risks of damage to the collections. Keeping the air circulation to avoid the stagnant air, cleaning for the maintenance of hygienic condition, periodic inspection of the collection to check well within limits and take remedial action to check the possible damage. The principles of Fumigation are as stated here. (i) The agent must be in vapor or gaseous phase and not present as an aerosol. (ii) The transient nature of fumigants indicate that there is no permanent pesticide effect and it does not prevent re-infestation. (iii)The fumigant effectiveness is to be developed in terms of concentration and time factors. (iv)The effects of temperature. (v)Selection of a proper fumigant. (vi) The problem of absorption by protein containing materials such as leather etc. which is most important must be taken into account. (vii) The safety of Operator is to be ensured. (viii) The disposal of the used fumigants from the Chamber must be controlled. This knowledge of sensitivity to each of these components has increased, restricting the choice of fumigants that can be used making the design of a safe facility which is more complex. There is a need for a Airflow requirements for fumigation booths so that there is a proper ventilation and toxic gases can be removed or diluted to a low enough level so that a safe atmosphere is present before re-entry is made in the booth. Fume extractors are the easy answer to take care of the problem, so that no harm is ensured for the Operators.

Moreover there is a interest among the conservators to find possible alternatives of the use of chemicals which pollute the environment so as to reduce health hazards for living beings .There are attempts to find out time tested indigenous herbs and natural products to take the place of the harmful chemicals and increase the level of pollution further. Traditionally there are many herbal and natural products which have been used in India for eradication of micro-organisms and to keep insects away from the collections of manuscripts and records. The composition and components need to be identified by using latest research in this respect going on all over the world. To give a specific example in this respect of international collaboration with the USA is the setting up of a herbal insecticide factory in collaboration with an U.S. company named Grace where derivatives of Neem plant product 'Neemix' is being manufactured in India at Timkur near Banglore. Besides this many repositories of manuscripts are wrapping their manuscripts in red cotton cloth as it saves them from further damage.

Research is going on in many US, Australian and British institutions to use inert atmosphere or oxygen free atmosphere or use of vacuum chambers and show cases /storage cases to repel the micro-organisms away so that to check their growth due to cutting off the supply of oxygen which would be needed by them to survive. This is the age of oxygen scavengers and using air tight cases for their storage and show cases to keep them safe from damaging agents. Attempts of using radiological methods of control have their own radiation hazards. Freezing is the most user friendly. It involves placing the insect or fungus infected manuscripts in an atmosphere of below freezing temperature. It is reported to kill all stages of life cycle of insects and fungus spores. Microwave irradiations are now ionizing radiations with frequency between 30MHz to 30Ghz. This type of irradiation does not produce any heat and the apparatus remains cold, but the object gets warmed. Paper manuscripts, palm leaf, parchment contains sufficient moisture 4-8%.therefore we can expose them to microwaves Flieder,et al,1995.Besides many examples of keeping the valuable documents of National importance in a sealed atmosphere having inert gas or in the vacuum sealed cases in which there is no oxygen. One example is that of the Declaration of Independence of the United States of America and the other being the Constitution of the Indian republic. These are two very well known of such examples. In general, spore forming bacteria are killed with short exposure while a longer exposure is required for 100% kill of spore forming bacteria. Library Congress Washington is of the view that comparatively high dose is required to destroy the bacterial infection than insect infestation.

5. PREPARATION OF THE CONDITION REPORT

Based on their scientific examination, visual and instrumental, a form for this purpose which was devised earlier and which would give full information on their condition. Main purpose of examination is to find out what are the vital factors on which the subsequent decision making is made. Before employing any conservation treatment documentation is essential since the future course of action would depend on it. The basic questions are (i) What is it? (ii) What is it made from? (iii) What is it's general condition? (iv) How much repair has been carried out in the past? (v) How dirty is it or what is the foreign material on it?

1. Examination of Physical factors.

Manuscripts are valuable to a society and, therefore, are to be preserved for as long as possible. Examination of an object as a preliminary to scientific conservation is a process of familiarization with the object and its structure giving on only as a knowledge.

(a) Visual examination. (b) Examination with hand lens. (c) Microscopic Examination. (d) Examination under visible and invisible lightings such as normal light, UV, IR and X rays.

2. Examination of Chemical factors.

(i) Chemical and micro chemical (ii) composition of materials. (iii) Action of solvents (Inorganic and organic). (iv) Solubility of various components (v) pH and (v) stains and their nature.

3. Examination of biological factors.

(a) Deposits left by insects and marks left by them. (b) Stains/Colour and nature of fungal growth. (c) Remainnents left by Biodeterioration.

A full description and condition report as well as photographs of the manuscript leaf by leaf before conservation and later after conservation is done to keep records of it's earlier condition and what treatments have been executed to leaf by leaf. The methods employed should be reported step by step and should include the precise chemical and procedures followed should be recorded faithfully for future reference of the Conservators. On which would base the future conservation needs. This information is included at appendix A. It would be seen from this that even a minute detail is recorded for any reference in future. (Appendix 1)

CONDITION REPORT:

Appendix 1

TREATMENT RECORD OF MANUSCRIPTS

Date Received : Examiner
Owner : Date of Return
Acc. No.
Subject
Author
Provenance
Period
Size
Painted/Unpainted
If a Volume
- (a) Number of pages
- (b) Number of illustrated pages
- (c) Bound/Unbound

Nature of Support
(a) Thickness
- (b) Wt./Sq.m
- (c) Layers used to make it
- (d) Identification of material
- (e) Sizing material
- (f) Others

Alteration in the support
- (a) Strength
- (b) Acidity/Alkalinity
- (c) Physical damage
- (d) Biological damage
- (e) Stains
- (f) Foxing
- (g) Colour change

(h) Fading of writing
(i) Others

Nature of Binding
(a) Type of binding
(b) Wt. per Sq. meter
(c) Nature of material

Alteration in the binding
(a) Strength
(b) Condition of covering Cloth/Board/ Leather
(c) Physical damage
(d) Biological damage
(e) Others

Photographic record
(a) Visible Light
(b) Ultraviolet Light
(c) Infra-red Light
(d) Xrays
(e) Macrophotograph
(f) Microphotograph
(g) Slide

Any other Observations

Treatment Proposed

6. VARIOUS PROCESS IN CONSERVATION

(a) Deacidification

The process of de-acidification involves the removal and neutralization of these acids from proper which is the most formidable factor to make paper yellow in colour, fragile and cause decay. (a) Dry Powders de-acidification (i) Finely precipitated chalk calcium carbonate or magnesia is sprayed over the document and is allowed to remain in contact for 36-48 hrs. (ii) Post lip tissue is reported to do the job containing magnesium acetate which neutralizes the acidity and also reinforces the fragile document besides it can do the lamination and de-acidification in one single operation. There are four main methods of de-acidification. (a) Aqueous de-acidification by (i) Immerssion methods (ii) Calcium hydroxide in water (1.5gms/ltand calcium bicarbonate in water (2gms/lt) (iii) leaching of chemicals used (iv) Barrow's Method magnesium (20gms) and calcium bicarbonate (2gms) added in one liter of water and carbon oxide gas is passed into it for overnight. Soluble magnesium bicarbonate and calcium bicarbonate gets converted in to respective insoluble carbonates, neutralizes the acidity and acts as future inhibitor of acidity followed by distilled solution of sodium carboxy methyl cellulose. Aqueous de-acidification is the process where water is used to remove acids. (a) Calcium hydroxide used along with calcium bi-carbonate (b) Magnesium bicarbonate (c) Non-aqueous (d) Vapor phase and (e) Solid phase de-acidification.

Advantages of aqueous method:-

(1) Removes water soluble acids. (2) Removes some spots and stains (3) Removes discolouring agents. (4) Regenerates the lost strength of the paper.

Disadvantages:-

(1) May affect water soluble inks, dyes & pigments if not fixed earlier.
(2) Each leaf needs to be treated individually so it is a time consuming and expensive.
(3) Not good option for fragile and broken documents which would need precautions during the wetting process and may not loose them.

(b) *Mass Deacidification*

Mass deadification process are the ones in which bulk of the books can be deacidified at the same time. This is cost effective and time saving proposition. Today there many mass-deacidification methods such as the following.

1. Diethyl Zinc process is one of the vapor phase method which has a chamber where books are kept vacuumed and nitrogen is filled in it where Diethyl Zink is flushed in which deacidifies books. Next step is to spray methanol so that it can absorb extra diethyl zinc. Once the operation is over books are kept in open for acclimatization.
2. Book saver process is in which books are kept in a vacuum chamber and ammonia gas is passed into it which deacidifies them. Ethylene gas is passed into it to absorb extra ammonia followed by keeping them in open for acclimatization.
3. Book keeper process is also a vapour phase process The chamber is evacuated to remove the air and nitrogen is stuffed followed by Magnesium oxide to interact.

   $MgO+H_2O \longrightarrow Mg(OH)_2$

   This Magnesium hydroxide neutralizes the acid.

   $Mg(OH)_2$+Acid forms a salt
4. Wei T'o process is an aqueous method-The chamber is made devoid of air, at 60 degree Celsius and books are kept at this temperature for 24hrs.Next,vacuum pressure of 2mm Hg is created. The methoxy magnesium methyl carbonate is given. Pressure is now reduced so that it can come to solution state and kept for 20 minutes thus deacdification is done.
5. French Process is a non aqueous method. Ethylates of magnesium and Titanium are used and a solution of cyclohexyl disiloxane. All oxides of magnesium and titanium .act as de acidifiers and extra material gets converted into $Mg\ CO_3$ acts as buffer.

6. British Library Process is also a non aqueous method. Ethyl acrylate and methyl metha acrylate are used in the ratio of 1:5. Solution used are dimethyl amino ethyl resulting into polymerization of these monomers takes place using energy from gamma rays (Cobalt 60).

Mass deacidification methods, focusing on the major developments in research and application of the main operational systems. This study is intended primarily to support the development of a well-considered preservation policy by librarians and archivists, with a focus on the practical implications of mass deacidification rather than the technical details of the deacidification process. The study provides a brief history of the development of the technical process, a condensed description of the treatment principle, an overview of available research and test results, indicating the main advantages and disadvantages of the process, and an inventory of actual applications for five mass deacidification systems: Several other initiatives are also described, involving large-scale rather than mass treatment technologies, and essentially combining deacidification with strengthening of paper. The main findings are discussed within the framework of a critical evaluation of the current possibilities and limitations of mass deacidification in general.

Goals of Mass Deacidification These are the results that the Library Congress expected of an ideal mass deacidification treatment in 1994.

- neutralize acidic paper and add an alkaline reserve.
- produce a pH value between 6.8 and 10.4 which is evenly distributed throughout the book.
- should not cause any damage to adhesives, inks or dyes.
- should not cause any odor or any change in the color of the paper.
- should not cause loss of pliancy or mechanical strength.

Faculty members of the Slovak University of Technology added these further requirements.

- the chemicals used have to be safe.
- the process has to be able to be applied to any kind of paper.
- the process can not cause swelling or warping of the paper.

The processes impart an adequately high pH in studies conducted by the European Commission on Preservation and Access, the Library of Congress, and a team of scientists from the Centre de Recherches sur la Conservation des Documents Graphiques in the early and mid-nineties. Book Keeper produced a pH of 9-10. CSC Book Saver gives a pH of 8.78-10.5. Wei T'o gives 7.5 to 10.4, and Paper save gives a pH of 7.5-9. The same studies also found that the processes had negative cosmetic side effects. Book Keeper left "a palpable residue", clamp marks on the covers, and caused some of the colored inks to rub off. CSC Book Saver left a "white powdery deposit" on books. Paper save caused "discoloration, white deposit, Newton rings, bleeding of inks and dyes, odor and different 'feel' of the paper." Wei T'o caused "odor, white residues, rings, cockling, (yellow) discolorations and adhesive bleeding."

However, these studies are now more than ten years old and several of the processes have changed their formulae since the mid-nineties. Conservators from the British Library acknowledge that the existing mass deacidification processes are still developing and further research needs to be conducted on their chemical and mechanical effects. The Library of Congress recommends libraries use mass deacidification to ensure that collections survive. Clearly, the conservators working for the Library of Congress believe that mass deacidification is vital to library collections, whatever the cosmetic effects may or may not be.

(c) *History of Mass Deacidification and Research*

Mass deacidification - along with microfilm and lamination was developed during the early- and mid-20th century as a response to the chemical process of hydrolysis which the fibers that constitute paper, providing its structure and strength, have their bonds broken, resulting in paper that becomes increasingly brittle over time. Environmental pollutants can react with paper to form acids that promote oxidation, creating more acid as a by-product, which results in a positive feedback loop of autocatalytic destruction. Supported in part by grants from the Council on Library Resources, William J. Barrow conducted research into paper decay and found that no more than three percent of the books published between 1900 and 1949 would survive more than fifty years. In response to this, the Standing Committee on the Preservation of Research Library Materials was formed by the Association of Research Libraries (ARL) in 1960.

Barrow also invented an aqueous process to neutralize acid in paper while depositing an alkaline buffer that would retard the rate of decay. In addition to Barrow's original method, both non-aqueous - employing organic solvents - and vaporous - the Library of Congress' DEZ (diethyl zinc) treatment - methods of achieving the same results have been researched in an attempt to reduce time, labor, and cost requirements. One technique proposed was to place books in an evacuated chamber, then introduce diethyl zinc(DEZ). In theory, the diethyl zinc reacts with acidic residues in the paper, leaving an alkaline residue that would protect the paper against further degradation. In practice, the heating required to remove trace water from the books before reaction (DEZ reacts violently with water) caused an accelerated degradation of the paper, and a range of other chemical reactions between DEZ and other components of the book (glues, bindings) caused further damage and the production of unpleasant smells. Regardless, in the 1980s, a pilot plant for mass deacidification using this process was constructed by NASA and was tested on books provided by the Library of Congress. However, it was discovered in 1986 that the DEZ had not been removed in one of the deacidification runs and was pooled in the bottom of the chamber, and probably remained within some of the plumbing. DEZ is violently flammable when it comes in contact with either oxygen or water vapor, so the vacuum chamber could not be opened to remove the books within. Eventually, explosives were used to rupture the suspect plumbing; suspicions of the presence of residual DEZ were confirmed by the subsequent fire that destroyed the plant.

The chemical company Akzo made later attempts at refining the process; though the risks of fire and explosions were reduced by better process design, damage and odour remained a problem. In the end, Akzo decided the process was not a viable commercial proposition, and shut down their research at the end of 1994.

While deacidification has been adopted by major research libraries such as the Library of Congress and the New York Public Library, it is not clear that many archives, particularly those in the United States, have followed suit. Whereas some European national archives have tested deacidification techniques, the United States' National Archives, which pioneered an aqueous technique that improved upon Barrow's, has chosen to invest its preservation dollars elsewhere. In 2000, the Chief of the NARA Document Conservation Laboratory defended the lack of a mass deacidification program by pointing to differences between library and archival collections, for example noting that many of the papers coming to NARA were of a higher quality than those in library collections; that the Archives does not receive records from Federal government agencies until they are at least 30 years old, by which time acidic paper will have already been irrevocably weakened; and that limited resources might best be applied elsewhere, such as climate control, as under the Archives' Twenty-Year Preservation Plan, the emphasis was on "maximum benefit for the greatest number of records."

(d) Bleaching

It has to depend on (i) If the colours or inks are soluble in water it should not be done (ii)It can be done with aqueous solutions if colours and inks are fast or ink can be fixed by using some fixatives (iii) If the colours and ink can not be fixed. Only a soft Eraser of special type can be used to do the job. Various chemicai bleaching solutions that are being used for the purpose at present are as following.

Simple de ionized water should be used to improve the look of the document.

(1) 1% Potassium per magnate and followed by 1% Citric acid.
(2) 5% Chloromine T in alcohol if the colours run in water otherwise aqueous solution in water may do the job
(3) 3% Calcium hypochlorite in water.
(4) 1% solution of Sodium chlorite and Formaldehyde, followed by washing in water to increase the pH
(5) Weak solution of Hydrogen per oxide (.5% to 1%).
(6) Sun bleaching.

Bleaching these days is considered very drastic and, therefore, the attempt is to improve the look of the document rather than making it new a fresh.

(e) Cleaning and Stain Removal

Spotted, stained or soiled documents need cleaning before any other treatment could be thought of.

(i) Mechanical Cleaning:-

Use of mechanical devices such as flattened spatula, soft erasers, brushing, air cleaning, synthetic erasing powders, bread crumbs.

(ii) Non aqueous cleaning:-

Chemicals such as acetone, benzene, carbon tetra chloride, petroleum ether, trichloro - ethylene and xylene etc.

(iii) Aqueous cleaning;-

Soaps, detergents and engymes (trypsin) and soap jelly are used.

(iv) Enzyme cleaning

Enzymes are complex organic substances which are naturally occurring proteins and can catalyze specific organic substances which can start or accelerate a chemical reaction into water soluble substances without taking part in it directly. Enzymes were once called as ferments such as yeast which is used in the production of alcohol. Enzymes have been characterized as below.

1. The main advantage of enzymes is it's specificity which enables only one kind of material such as starch or protein to be acted on and rapidity of action, meaning that only short immersion periods are desireable.
2. The acidity or alkalinity of the solution in which enzymes are used is also specific. The incorrect acidity or alkalinity may also destroy the enzymes or make them inactive, therefore, an optimum pH is required.
3. There is an optimum temperature for the use of each particular enzyme and therefore, the enzymes were to be stored at low temperature in a refrigerator. The enzymes get destroyed at high temperature above 37 degree centigrade.
4. The enzymes after doing their job must be washed or inactivated by using alcohol or ethanol.

RESTORATION

1. Repair and strengthening of decayed manuscripts.

After fumigation, cleaning, examination, documentation, neutralization of acidity, it comes to add physical strength to the decayed leaf what is needed is to evaluate the necessity for such a task. In some of the manuscripts first few leaves or end sheet might have become loose. These will often need full reinforcement with tissue. Physical strength of a manuscript leaf becomes unavoidable when it is found that leaf can not be handled without further loss in any form and becomes necessary to strengthen it. There are many aspects of this problem and the follow up treatment should be first evaluated. This would depend on many thoughtful decisions. For this purpose one has to decide all proposed action to be formulated first which would vary from case to case. Manuscripts are structurally if illustrated are complex documents, valuable for their form, materials and content. Balancing the requirements of preservation and access to them is often very challenging, requiring research across a range of cultural and material issues. As well as studying manufacturing techniques, it is also necessary to integrate traditional knowledge about the care of manuscripts with current conservation practices. Working with international experts in the field and Muslim community groups, the University of Melbourne's Centre for Cultural Materials Conservation has developed protocols for handling, display and storage of the Middle Eastern Manuscripts Collection. The collection is stored in a pristine, environmentally controlled environment, and Qurans' are stored physically above secular texts.

2. *Strengthening of Leaves*

1. The hair line tears need to be mended with pulp made of all cellulose tissue paper using an adhesive like methyl cellulose which has low rate of shrinkage after drying.
2. Losses in the shape of holes, broken corners and missing parts can also be restored / made up by using pulp as mentioned earlier or acid free tissue after chamfering of the edges of the same thickness as the original. Adhesive has been the methyl cellulose or C.M.C. or starch paste.
3. In the case of leaf damaged at the edges we can do Strip lining and if the leaf is very fragile, brittle we may do full lining with acid free

and Japanese tissue paper using methyl cellulose or gluten free starch paste as an adhesive or lignin free.

4. Tissue lamination can also be attempted with a highly transparent tissue imported from Japan (3.6 G.S.M.) and starch paste or methyl cellulose.
5. Solvent lamination or hand lamination or cold lamination using cellulose acetate foil, acetone and fine grade tissue can be done provided it has been ensured that document is now acid free and the de-acidification has been done prior to lamination very near to pH 7. There was a time in the history of lamination when the solvent lamination was termed as Indian method of lamination during fifties/ sixties of the last century. Lamination was once the method of choice for preservation of paper records, documents, manuscript all over the globe. Machine lamination introduced in by the British Library and Australian Library used heat sealing lamination as the laminate was having a coating. The heat melts the adhesive which was coated on a plastic laminate (Cellulose Tri Acetate) has a melting point 60-70 degree centigrade for 2 minutes which is least damaging for the original material being laminated. We in the National Museum, New Delhi also acquired the Morane Laminator after my training in Australia(1960-61). This sheet has an adhesive coating and it could be delaminated by putting the sheet in alcohol. The main difficulty about solvent Acetate lamination is being highlighted now whether it can be delaminated safely or not and reversibility is still possible after three decades.

3. *Chiffon Lamination*

A layer of thin but strong silk tissue applied to mend or strengthen a leaf or other documents printed or other supports described above is called chiffon silk lamination. Chiffon is a very transparent silk which originated first in France from the word 'chffre' meaning rag. Starch paste was used in this chiffon lamination. Unfortunately there have been many problems related to this technique. In India it is being used in large scale and I hope our NRLC would also evaluate this technique as it is doing the evaluation of Acetate lamination. They should come forward with authentic study based on documentation done by the Conservators in the past. I think where ever (1) PVC film has been used there we can expect this problem (2) If the neutralization has not been done fully before lamination of the document (3) Wherever the records have not been left by the conservators in the past of the treatment done or (4) Present techniques of evaluation of acetic acid incrased content now present are not sure. I have a hunch that the documents showing large quantity of acetic acid present at this point in time, in those documents, which have been laminated with cellulose acetate foil or by some other foil having acetate in one form or the other. I can surely give my option to be against PVC but we need an elaborate study before we discard cellulose acetate lamination out right. I am convinced that lamination is not the panacea and even a document such as the priceless documents as the emancipation proclamation were laminated. Heat and pressure lamination may damage the already damaged documents resulting to darkening of the document to some extent, I agree. Lamination of properly de-acidified documents using acetone with hand and cotton swab. I do not agree outright and unless researched adequately by a competent laboratory who have enough practical conservation experience would do full justice for or against, without any bias. I remember the NRLC reported use of PVA in the past but the ASI did not agree having used on the marble surface of Taj any time. Had there been available the full documentation done at the time of conservation we could come to a definite conclusion accordingly.

Ever since the lamination process was developed and many attempts have been reported to improve the techniques all over the world. The National bureau of Standards eventually made an attempt to standardize lamination, recommending a process with several stages. We have to take care of the acidity inherent in a particular paper, cellulose acetate, the tissue paper, the composition of chiffon and lastly the plasticizer to keep the elasticity/

flexibility intact under different conditions of temperature and humidity. The purchase of cellulose film through the National Archives of India and urge to lamination prompted many other institutions in India and the nearby countries made it apparently acceptable to all. Some of the institutions are continuing the lamination of documents. Some are doing lamination of documents with chiffon using starch paste but some have switched over to CMC or Methyl cellulose in place of starch paste. In addition, laminated documents often have aesthetic problem for the visitors and the art historians. There may be some inherent causes present in the documents themselves. Prior de-acidification before lamination is the source of worry, since the layers of plastic encasing the document may trap acids within the laminate causing the document to yellow to brown and may give smell of acetic acid turning the document very brittle. Badly torn documents which have been repaired locally with sub standard materials will aggravate the already grave situation further. The use of heat and pressure may start chemical reactions while the sealed layers of laminate would trap the by products creating a harmful microclimate for the document. When the plastic film begins to break down the one who would suffer would be the document. The bonds of the cellulose acetate molecule would break down releasing the acetic acid. This is particularly troublesome for the binding process since it would place considerable stress on the bound edge of the document. Once this degradation process begins, damage will only become worse with time. This has forced the Conservators to resort to many new processes mentioned here after.

4. *Encapsulation, Tissue paper lamination and Leaf casting*

Encapsulation i.e. encasing and then sealing the document in between two sheets of polyester (Mylar film-type D) to protect a frequently handled, fragile exhibit piece. When all the leaves in a book are extremely weak and/or brittle and require overall support, encapsulation with the polyester film and post-binding is the best solution. Each leaf of the book is placed between two sheets of polyester film, and the film is sealed along the four edges. Polyester is a category of polymers more specifically condensation polymers, which contain the ester functional group in their main chain. If the leaves are still in the folio form, the folios will usually need to be cut along the fold to felicitate encapsulation. Polyester film has an electrostatic charge. This is however, not recommended for leaves that become have loose, flaking or friable media because the electrostatic charge may harm the leaf further. To-day, encapsulation within acid free sheet protectors has made the preservation process more efficient. This process rightly superior than the lamination. The documents simply float freely and can be easily removed if wanted. I do remember I gave a practical demonstration of this technique during a workshop on conservation of paper documents by using encapsulation about a decade back to the participants of a workship held at the Victoria Memorial Hall, Kolkata.

5. *Leaf Casting*

It is another method of strengthening the decayed leaves. Measured amount of acid free pulp according to the loss in a sheet of paper, it's thickness, it's size is introduced in the form of a fine fibrous layer under vaccum suction arrangement Leaf Caster. This reinforces the leaf which is later air dried or kept on a drying table especially designed for the purpose.

6. *Tissue Paper Lamination*

An acid free flax fiber tissue paper of pure white colour, filled with approximately 18-20% calcium carbonate. Because of it's exceptionally high alkaline reserve, this paper offers maximum protection against acid migration of pH value minimum of 8.0. Tissue paper lamination is widely practiced as it is the time tested harmless method of mending/repairing of paper documents. Conservators removed previous lamination in repeated solvent baths of acetone and removed the old mends. The re-mending can be easily done with the time tested acid free tissue strips using starch paste which can be easily undone by using simple water. Japanese Tissue fine grade, it being the transparent most of 3.6 G.S.M. grade has to be used keeping the transparency in mind and best quality of the results. Some conservators prefer to use methyl cellulose as adhesive.

7 *Lamination*

Some quarters in the conservation field are over concerned about the manuscripts laminated by the Indian method of solvent lamination. There findings are alarming and have openly criticized the technique which brought it on the world map. This needs proper evaluation of the so called unusual problem. In view of the lack of written documentation in cases where lamination has been done. It is being projected that such manuscripts are deteriorating because of the increase in the acid content.

Content has supposed to have increased many fold because of the cellulose acetate having been used in this process has degraded chemically and has produced further acidity in the manuscript which can be smelt with the smell of acetic acid coming from the laminated documents. We must ponder the various reasons for this change and come to definite conclusions to check the problem and its reasons. A committee may be formed of the practical conservationists and conservation scientists to study and know the exact reasons for this strange but urgent problem with open mind and taking care of the pros and cones of the situation sooner the better.

Lamination per se is purely a mechanical process for conferring adequate strength to the brittle and fragile documents, but it in itself does not do any thing to remove and neutralize the increase in the acidity content. The point I am having in my mind that is there any way to know whether the acidity of the document was neutralized fully before laminating the document or this is the case of acidity being increased in the trapped micro environment of the manuscript. The problem can not be solved unless we have correct reasons for it. This acid deterioration would surely continue and even increase after lamination if de acidification prior to lamination has not been done satisfactorily especially in the tropical climatic condition of increase in temperature and high humidity being trapped inside the assembly. This, therefore means that a process of deacidification prior to lamination should be regarded as an essential and crucial factor in controlling the insidious degradation induced in the document by acids. A study of the practical aspects of this problem was first visualized by Barrow in 1943 and therefore he advocated which involved two stages; the document was first immersed in a saturated solution of calcium hydroxide (lime water) and then in a dilute 0.15% solution of calcium bicarbonate. Later this process was simplified so that deacidification could be carried out thus avoiding the need to take the book apart and treat each leaf individually in one stage using only a solution of magnesium bicarbonate. He suggested that the pH of the deacidified document should be slightly alkaline pH 7.5. At the same time a deposit of either calcium or magnesium carbonate is left in the fibers of the document where it can act as a buffer against extrinsic sources of acidity, such as sulphur di oxide. Here comes the point in support of non-aqueous techniques of deacidification since the documents in which ink is soluble in aqueous solutions can not be treated this way. A dilute solution of crystalline barium hydroxide ($Ba(OH)_2.8\ H_2O$) in methyl alcohol and then hung up to dry in the air. Any excess of barium hydroxide is converted by the carbon dioxide in the air into barium carbonate, which gets deposited in the fibres of paper etc..

It is well known that the physical and chemical properties of paper and other allied materials tend to alter with time i.e. all the materials change with age. This ageing results in deterioration of mechanical strength which becomes weak and brittle. It is therefore necessary to reinforce them so that these could be handled safely. The classical method for reinforcements of manuscripts and documents was done by a manual process, in which either an open weave silk fabric (chiffon or crepeline) or tissue paper using adhesive made from starch, dextrin or flour. This process of strengthening has been extensively used since the end of the 19th century, but it does have certain drawbacks. A new process of reinforcement came into use which is referred as Lamination. This is a process in which the document is embedded between sheets of a synthetic plastic film and/ or tissue. There has been considerable controversy among archivists and conservators about this technique of lamination; doubts have been expressed about the efficacy of the process and the possible deleterious effects of the new synthetic materials on the documents. This report on the lamination of documents has been conducted by A.E. Werner to survey the pros and cone of this process called Lamination., and it's advantages and disadvantages. The question of the deacidification which is a very important factor in the preservation of materials in question. From the practical point of view this can be divided into three main processes. (1) Dry mounting, (2) Heat sealing and (3) Solvent lamination.

(1) Dry Mounting:- The cellulose tri acetate pre coated with a pressure-sensitive adhesive which attaches the film to the document at a low temperature and with a moderate pressure. When I was in Australia in the years 1960-61 on a Commonwealth Fellowship in the restoration field I saw the machine and its working being used in the New South Wales Library, Sydney. The method outwardly was worth considering to be adopted in the conservation Department of the National Museum, New Delhi. We imported the Morane Laminator from the Morane Plastic Co. Ltd., Ashford, Middlesex, England, UK and we used it for lamination of the Birch bark manuscripts leaves after the consolidation of the separating layers of the sheets, dry brushing & chemical cleaning of surface deposits and stains. Cellulose tri acetate film which gave a semi matt finish was acceptable for archival materials more so for the reason that it could be delaminated easily in rectified spirit. The process of lamination is carried out by placing the document between two sheets of the plastic film and appling a slight pressure at about 70-80 degree centigrade. It works on the same principle as of a Photographic dry mounting press or even can be tacked with a little warm electric iron which should be having a thermostatic controll.

Other dry mounting methods such as Mipofolie genotherm process, Post lip duplex process and Dispro process were discarded by us for one reason or the other e.g. poly vinyl chloride and polyvinyl acetate film with an acrylate resin. The chemicals used for the de lamination which have an adverse reaction with the natural adhesive present in the layers of it need not to be used.

8. *Solvent Lamination*

Barrow's laminator which was imported by the National Archives of India in early fifties and which was initially used, had the disadvantage of heat and pressure which the fragile documents and manuscript leaves could not be used in case of historic documents. It was, therefore, thought proper to be used for maps and charts etc. with good results. Solvent lamination thus had it's beginning in India and was also called as Indian method of Lamination with success. The first of these was evolved in the National Archives of India in 1955 by Late Shri O.P. Goel and later supported by Late Shri Y.P. Kathpalia, both of them were working in the National Archives of India, New Delhi. This did bring India on a strong footings since the method was named as Indian method of Lamination.

In this process the document was covered on one side with a film of cellulose acetate over which is placed a sheet of fine Japanese tissue paper. The surface was then rubbed with a swab of cotton wool moistened with acetone and smoothened with the swab or a roller. The process becomes easy with practice. This Indian method was acknowledged by experts from abroad. The most significant feature of this technique is the fact that the document is not subjected to increased temperature and pressure during lamination, a factor which is of prime importance when the lamination of the fragile or valuable documents are concerned. The Indian method of solvent lamination has been adopted by the Canadian Archives in Ottawa and the U.S. National Archives in Washington for the lamination of documents and which could not be treated by any other method of lamination

9. *Evaluation of Lamination*

The criteria which an ideal lamination process should fulfill as regards the materials used (the laminating film and adhesive), and the actual method of lamination. Film should possess the following properties.

(a) It should be inherently stable i.e. show long term resistance to degradation when exposed to any environmental conditions to be expected under normal conditions
(b) It should be flexible and resistant to abrasion so that it can withstand the normal handling that documents receive in use.
(c) It should confer considerable increase in strength on the document it is meant to protect and at the same time be as thin as possible.
(d) It should not interfere with the legibility of the document.
(e) It should not contain any additives which might leach out and have a deleterious effect on document.
(f) It should be possible to attach the film to the document with the minimum of effort.
(g) It should be possible to remove the film, if necessary, by a simple method which will not damage the document.

Indian method of Lamination is basically a mechanical process for providing the adequate strength to the brittle and fragile documents, but it does nothing to remove or neutralize the acidity that is known to be the major factor responsible for the brittleness of the document. It would be highly desirable to have a process in which lamination and deacidification could be achieved in a simple operation. A first attempt in this direction has been made in the Post lip duplex method of lamination but a detailed evaluation has to be done of it's efficacy in long run. In view of the recent development the matter raised should be resolved with out any loss of time.

10. Binding of those Manuscripts which were bound earlier

Due to stress and strain experienced by the manuscript because of it's use the binding becomes loose and the leaves may get detached from it and outermost sections may become loose. In such cases loose sections can be oversewn and the assembly made tight by applying adhesive like Mowicol acid free. To the loose leaves at the spine and resetting the whole manuscript. New fly leaves can be rejoined and new pasting done with the board which should be acid free. The torn backing cloth can be reinforced by pasting new calico cloth slips to match the colour of the old covering and the fore ends can also be likewise reinforced. In those cases where the binding is in the advance stage of decay, it is preferred to do rebinding to avoid any further damage to the text. Care should be taken to refix the old noting done on it.

The craft of book binding originated in India, where religious sutras were copied on to palm leaves (cut into two, lengthwise) with a metal stylus. There are a large number of Arabic and Persian manuscripts in the collection of the National Museum, New Delhi which have been acquired by it's Art Purchase Committee every year from open press advertisement after Indian Independence first when it was temporarily housed in the Rastrapati Bhavan and later after December 1960 once it's own building was officially inaugurated and opened for public view by the then President of India.

Books requiring conservation treatment run the gamut from the very earliest of texts to books with modern bindings that have undergone heavy usage. For each book, the conservator must choose a course of treatment that takes into account the book's value, whether it comes with the binding, the text, the provenance, or some combination of the three. Many professional book and paper conservators in the United States are members of the American Institute for Conservation of Historic and Artistic Works (AIC), whose guidelines, set forth in the AIC's Code of Ethics are generally considered to outline an appropriate approach to the treatment of rare or valuable materials.

In restoration of hand binding, the pages and book covers are often hundreds of years old, and the handling of these pages has to be undertaken with great care and a delicate hand. The binding archival process can extend a book's life for many decades and is necessary to preserve books that sometimes are limited to a small handful of remaining copies worldwide. The first step in saving and preserving a book is its deconstruction. The text need to be separated from the covers and, only if necessary, the stitching removed. This is done as delicately as possible. Leaf by leaf restoration is done at this point in time, be it the removal of foxing, ink stains, tears in pages, etc. Various techniques are employed to repair the various types of leaf damage that might have occurred during the life of the book.

Red-Rot affected leather bindings become crumbly and would need consolidation by introducing a resinous binder. In 19th cent. starch rubbing followed by application of a layer of glue. For use as adhesive for the binding, some laboratories are using Plaintex based on ethyl acralate which is dissolved in hydrocarbons and has been used for consolidation of decayed leather binding. One part of it is mixed with three parts of Trichloro ethane. Which is used for consolidation on leather and is reported reversible. Polyurethane dissolved in hydrocarbons was also used for fixing the loose leather flakes of the leather.

Chapter Five

STEPS IN CONSERVATION OF SPECIFIC MATERIALS

PALM LEAF MANUSCRIPTS

After preparing the condition report, studying the nature of materials used in it's making and the treatment it needs to keep it in good condition besides understanding the future preventive steps to be taken which we know now and what is appropriate for it's physical well being for as long as possible. The Sri tala variety, thin and smooth on which the writings have been done behave like paper manuscript in which ink has been used or paint has been used for making a picture where it may need fixing of the loose or flaking colours by using a fixative such as a 5% poly vinyl acetate or modern polymers. The physical losses have to be restored to strengthen it so that it could be handled properly. If there are any insect holes or irregular missing portions in it we do tissue or chiffon lamination using starch or methyl cellulose paste. Holes for tying the leaves together by passing a cord through these holes after mending them so that these do not get bigger and bigger after use and alternately finding a new position for the hole. The general techniques have been mentioned earlier in solvent cleaning or separation of the stuck leaves by putting them in above solutions along with an insecticide and followed by gentle separation using a Scalpel. The regaining of the lost flexibility of palm leaves can be achieved by using an oil such as citronella or camphor oil. at times a mixture of citronella oil and water (1;1) helps. Reinking of the Tala variety of Palm leaves can be done in conjunction with step suggested above by sprinkling carbon powdwer to go into the incised areas and extra carbon from the surface can later be removed with a cotton swab dipped in alcohol. For strengthening, tissuing or backing with chiffon could be done as the case may be. Some times we may resort to suitable lamination if there is no other alternative. In case lamination of any kind is to be avoided encapsulation could be done between transparent sheets of Polyester or polyethylene or polypropylene using a tape to seal the edges or we may think of Leaf Casting.

Second category of palm leaf which is a thicker variety from South India and in which engraving has been done to write as well as pictures have been drawn and later filled with lamp black or charcoal powder has been sprinkled on\ the oiled palm leaves which makes them to stick to the body of the leaf and the text or drawing becomes clear. Thicker variety of palm leaf is mended with palm leaf by filling the losses and mending the edges. Flexibility is restored by oiling the leaves with Citronella oil. Tissue lamination helps in the strengthening of these leaves. We do not recommend to bind the leaves and prefer to keep them loose for making their study more comfortable. In India when the leaves have lost edges in the past are restored by integrating the lost areas with pieces of seasoned palm leaf of the same shape, size, thickness and colour. The joining of the matching pieces with original leaf is done with methyl cellulose or CMC keeping in view of the texture and the thickness of the leaf. Tiny holes in the leaf were filled using a pulp made from the acid free and lignin free tissue after making pulp of this material to give a compatible texture and material to the lost areas. The filled areas were then retouched with water or poster colours which ever matches with its original tone. As regards Sanchi pat manuscripts they can be safeguarded as in the case of Tala Palm leaf manuscripts.

BIRCH BARK MANUSCRIPTS

Birch Bark: Thymol fumigation in case of fungus affected leaves can help. ii. Cleaning of leaf by leaf with dry brushing or with solvents such as discussed elsewhere in this context. Separation of stuck up leaves we can try a softening agent and mild pressure. In case the ink is tested soluble in aqueous softening agent we may use molten paraffin oil to soften/relax them followed by drying or cleaning them one by one for excess of wax chemically. If some of the leaves have aseparating tendency of layers we may use CMC or starch paste to put them back in their proper position. PVA 3-5% can help in fixing the loose ink or pigments. In case the leaves are quite strong in the center but are broken or having the edges brittle and fragile The edges may be provided strip lining of following the contours of the loss of leaves. Leaves may be strengthened with chiffon or fine tissue lamination on one side or may be on both sides. Some workers prefer chiffon lamination using methyl cellulose or carboxi methyl cellulose. In case nothing proves to be of merit only resort is encapsulation as suggested earlier.

The Birch Bark manuscript may have a specific problem of it's layers having a tendency of getting apart which normally is not seen in most of the manuscript leaves on other materials. Layers of birch bark get separated while cleaning is attempted to clean the birch bark using acetone, ethanol and ether. ETOH along with CCL, acetone and citronela oil(1:1:1:1) makes the birch bark very soft, It does not separate the leaves. Loss in weight on cleaning is 9.3 and there is no drastic change in brightness (40 to 38). ETOH with triethanolamine (10%) 1:1:1 makes it very soft and oily. it does not separate the layers and the loss in weight is minimum though the brightness gets reduced from 44 to 33 which is not suitable. After fixing the separated parts of the leaf at their original places using carboxy methyl cellulose paste of required consistency 1% and a Japanese tissue paper after chamfering its edges so as to match with the contours of the gap to have a strong bond. If the layers are having a separating tendency, these could be fixed back at their respective positions by applying Methyl cellulose with a soft brush, to stick them with it's original position with the layer adjoining to it. This is followed by cleaning with cold water. Some obstinate stains can be removed by using 1% chloramines T. I feel it is very safe to resort to encapsulation since there is no risk involved to remove it without any chemical help and undertake any urgent treatment if need be. Samples so done two decade back are still in good condition.

PAPER MANUSCRIPTS

Paper manuscripts we find before the Moguls in the western Indian states like Gujarat, part of Maharastra and Rajasthan. The paper which was used here must have been imported from Arabian or it came with the travelers from their source country. They do not have any similarity with the manuscripts of the Mogul period. Their conservation is simple in nature. Manuscripts on paper especially the Persian and Arabic ones, the tradition of which reached India after the Mogul rule along with which Artists were brought from Persia and employed them in their courts and many art workshops were thus started functioning in India, who taught these Indian artists how to make manuscripts in the Persian, Arabic and middle eastern styles. They taught them which is the best paper to make manuscripts. There was an inner frame which was fixed within the outer frame. Usually the meeting point of their boundaries of the two frames were demarcated by colour boundary by verdigris a brilliant green *hasiya*. These manuscripts were written on the both side of the sheet and were occasionally illuminated by a beautiful miniature. The green colour *hasiya* was reported to be basic copper acetate and which very frequently damaged the paper at the points of it's contact since the pH was lower than 7 suggesting a change in its chemical structure from basic to acidic. One of our Iranian students who did her Masters with NMI did further research in this aspect for her Doctorate degree as she found it very peculiar happening with these Persian style manuscript which were executed in India. She found out after her study that the verdigris or *Zangal* used in Iran was mixed with saffron (*Keshar* in Hindi and *Zaffraan* in Urdu) and this buffer material, according to her made the difference in their behavior in Indian and Persian manuscripts.

This in my opinion that it was kept by those artists a guarded secret or saffron was not mixed with the verdigris. To me, it seems that though saffron was abundantly produced in Kashmir and must have been taken by them home on their return or it might have been earlier imported from France, Italy and Spain which was mixed by the artists as buffer. It is reported that most of them are copies of their Arabian and Persian originals. Some of the important manuscripts in the collection of the National Museum, New Delhi are Jain Kalpashutra, Sahnama Firdoshi (c-16th cent.AD), a Persian manuscript of by Abul Kasim Mansoor, History of Iran written in Nastalik script belonging to the 10th cent. and witten in Harat having some illustrations by Shiraj school of paintings. Very important copies of Persian manuscripts like Babar Nama, Aine- Akabari, Tujke –Jahangiri, Holi Quran and Asrarul-khat besides other copies which were acquired for the collection of the National Museum, New Delhi in 1961 Art Purchase Committee. A large number of Sanskrit manuscripts were also acquired. Dated manuscripts elaborate Indian History with authoritative authenticity. The manuscripts are from the 7th century to the 19th century. An interesting sample of Arabic and Persian manuscripts contribute to the library's non-European holdings and includes among other works several nineteenth century copies of the Qur'an, a sixteenth century copy of the *Rubay-iyat* of Omar Khayyam, 'Ali ibn Ani Talib's *Kitab nahj' al-balaghah* (1662), the "Diary of a journey from Ḍamascus to Istanbul" (1768), the G*ulistan-I Sa'di* (1799) and Huseyin ibn Isma'il's *Mecu'a-'I Vefeyat* (1919).

The Palm leaf was then dried and rubbed with ink, which would form a stain in the lower areas. The finished leaves were given numbers, and two long twines were threaded through each end through wooden boards. When closed, the excess twine would be wrapped around the boards to protect the leaves of the book. Buddhist monks took the idea through Persia, Afghanistan, and Iran, to China in the first century BC. Western writers at this point of time wrote longer texts as scrolls, and these were stored in shelving with small cubbyholes, similar to a modern wine rack. The word *volume*, from the Latin word *volvere* ("to roll"), comes from these scrolls. Court records and notes were written on tree bark and leaves, while important documents were written on papyrus. The modern English word *book* comes from the Proto-Germanic **bokiz*, referring to the beech wood on which early written works were recorded.

LEATHER BOOK BINDINGS

Decay of leather book bindings is brought about by a variety of causes. Traces of SO_2 present are absorbed by the leather and are ultimately converted into non-volatile H_2SO_4 which then begins to attack leather. This rotting can be caused by H_2SO_4 if during tanning the natural salts are removed. If the manuscript has an old binding which has decayed, it has to be de bound very carefully by cutting the stitches to separate the leaves, the old decayed board from the front as well as back and the cover on its front and back has to be detached to clean the deposits and restore the damaged portions to improve its look. The numbering of the pages has to be done before hand so that we do not disturb the sequence of the pages. It has been our experience that the leaves are mostly fragile damaged near the spine side or there is no margin left to accommodate the new binding or it is damaged badly on all sides. Strip lining may be necessary to restore the decayed edges and the guard are duly provided for new binding by using a synthetic adhesive and tissue paper of almost the same thickness and composition duly toned to match with the colour of the old leaf. According to the Venice charter, Article 12 “The replacements of missing parts must integrate harmoniously with the whole, but at the same time must be distinguishable from the original so that restoration does not falsify the artistic and historic evidence.” Venice Charter, Article 16: says” In all works of preservation, restoration or conservation there should always be precise documentation in the form of analytical and critical reports, illustrated with drawing and photographs Farmars with seal of the Empire were also very much in vouge during Moghals.

Every stage of work of cleaning, consolidation and arrangement as well as integration as well as technical and formal features identified during the course of work should be included. This record should be placed in the

Archives of a public institution and made available to research workers. It is recommended that the report should be published."

When the leather book bindings becomes dry and desiccated due to lack of moisture content, they need restoration of their flexibility by mere conditioning them i.e. by humidifying them followed by storing them in controlled RH so that moisture thus gained by them is not lost. Dressing may also be applied to the dry leather binding by lubricating their surface. However, consolidation of the leather by keeping it for three-four days in a room with 70-75% RH which would help improve the flexibility by increasing their bound water of the polar groups of protein molecules of the leather fibers known as it's hydration level. Lubricants help in such cases. British Leather Dressing mixture, PEG treatment, glycerin treatment, Bavon treatment with some oils. A systematic arrangement of pages after their treatment and restoration as discussed earlier in groups *(jujbandi)* of 8 or 16 pages has to be completed first. Board and the leather covering on the top has also to be restored.

Composition of BLD is as follows:-

1. Anhydrous lanolin ______________200 gm.
2. Cedar wood oil _________________ 30 ml.
3. Bees wax _________________________ 15 gm.
4. Diethyl ether ________________________ 350 ml

    Or

    Hexane ________________________________ 330 ml.

Leather containing waxy and greasy constitutents which gradually volatilize in hot climate and thus it looses its flexibility in course of time.

The National Museum, New Delhi has been following the B.L.D. as recommended by the British Museum, London.

(a) Leather Dressing by National Archives of India

The National Archives of India has been using the following mixture of the leather dressing.

(b) Dressing

Lanoline anhydrous	18 parts by weight
Bees Wax	1 part by weight
Cedar Wood Oil	2 parts by weight
Benzene	22 parts by weight

Since residual acidity in leather or in the atmosphere is injurious to it and accelerates it's decay, treatment of leather with a buffer salt potassium lactate (7% acqueous solution) or sodium benezoate (2-3% acqueous solution) is recommended before application of preservative dressing.

Some Conservators prefer the following mixture:-

(a)	Lanolin (anhydrous)	35%
(b)	Bees Wax	25%
(c)	Toluene	20%
(d	Poly vinyl Acetate 20%	10%
(e)	Solution of potassium lactate 7%, para-nitrophenol.25%	8.5%
(f)	Sodium chloride	.5%
(f)	Sodium pyrophosphate	1%
	Total 100%	

(c) Restoration of bindings

Restoration of the leather support, cuts and tears with compatible materials. BEVA 371 film can be simply scooped in with a heated Spatula as a film material into the area of loss. A skillful Worker knows what I mean. Bulked resins such as Acroloid F-10 and Plintex could also be used in many cases. Dring inserts can also be used by mixing them with the filling materials taking care of the tanning process accordingly. The restoration of Leather has gone a long way over the years with the advancement of science and technological Research.

The procedure is that the BLDs should be heated together first (bees wax can be omitted, its function is to act as a polish) and then the molten liquid is poured into the ether or hexane. The mixture should be allowed to cool while constantly stirring but cautiously as it is inflammable. The dressing should be applied sparingly and then rubbed well. It should be treated with soft cloth after two days. It darkens the leather but it is a treatment with good success record.

A CASE STUDY OF RESTORATION

(a) Restoration of Saha-Nama

As stated earlier, the Saha-Nama- a Persian Manuscript in the collection of the National Museum, New Delhi which has over 200 leaves except the illustrated leaves was in a very bad condition as a large number of them had separated from the adjoining separated sheets. The spine of the manuscript was separated by cutting the threads used for joining them at one time. This was primarily because of the use of a green pigment Basic Copper Acetate which had damaged the juncture of borders between the leaves which was demarcated the painted and unpainted areas. Since the paper as a whole was in good condition and strong enough it was adequate to strengthen the damage portions by using strips of Japanese fine tissue which was most suitable for the purpose since it was transparent and starch paste after neutralizing the acidity which was pH 5. The acidity was neutralized by using 10% Calcium hydroxide as it was quite satisfactory since it had no adverse effect on the ink as well as pigments. Paper strips as stated above were given on one side first and then the leaf was turned over and the similar strips were provided on this side also to avoid distortion of the leaf.

The individual leaf was allowed to dry on a glass sheet keeping a Milinex (Polyester) sheet just to ensure that the leaf does not stick to the table. However, tissue lamination was done on both sides of the text as an extra precaution for the leaves. The leaf once fully dry was removed from the table and kept under pressure so as to avoid distortion. Guards were provided on the left side and joined as these earlier. In this way all the leaves were restored and the manuscript was bound as a book in its original style. Individual sections were thus made and arranged in original scheme of joining them in groups. Stitching in groups (*Jugebandi*) were stitched as earlier. After stitching both sides were covered with acid free board using the help of a good quality hand made paper and using acid free Mowilith PVA emulsion the whole assembly is allowed to dry in a Book Binder's Press and its edges are made a little bigger binding cloth or leather is fixed in a set procedure as shown in the illustration below. This is one example mentioned here besides many other examples of restoration of Persian and Arabic manuscript which were restored with the help of the Technical Restorers/Binders who have retired now such as S. Shri Prem Chand, Bhawani Dutt, Prem Singh, Om Prakash Kalara and some others, when I was the Chief Restorer and the Head of the Conservation Department of the National Museum, New Delhi. Cover page Jacket I presume Research in this direction should be conducted to achieve the best results.

(b) Repair of Palm Leaves

The lost edges of the leaves have to be restored by integrating the lost areas with pieces of seasoned palm leaves of the same shape, size, thickness and colour. The joining of the matching pieces with original leaf was done with polymer adhesive keeping in view the texture and the thickness of palm leaf. Tiny holes of insects in some folios, were filled using cellulose fibres and cellulose adhesive in order to give a compatible texture and material to the damaged areas. The filled areas were later retouched with a matching tone to match the original. The broken holes in the center were filled with using the method of reintegration with a seasoned piece of leaf at the center and then a new hole was punched at the center according to the thickness of the new cotton cord that was used in place of the original damaged cord that could not hold the leaves together.

DIGITAL CONSERVATION

As stated earlier that with the advancement & in the development of writing technology, the Digital preservations with the help of which we can record and preserve the information as well as the pictorials after recording them on a magnetic tapes. We have already lost a lot of important historical and cultural testaments of our past due to neglect, ignorance of proper technology and lack of infrastructural facilities in terms of availability of trained men and proper equipment. Due to these reasons a lot of information has been lost, as these tapes are not directly accessible to the general public like other archival media (manuscripts, documents and photographs etc.) since availability of any interface media could magnify, translate, convert or transcribe the valuable information and can make the thus preserved information available to human (Audio cassette player is an interface media that convert the magnetic coding in to sound).

Indian archives are very good with the conservation of print media and photographic media and conservation of media tapes is on back foot. In some of the government archives and related institutions their number being small, not much work has been done for the Audio-Video tapes. Digital boom has already replaced the major market of audio and video tapes with different digital media storage devices like DVDs, CDs, Data Travelers etc. Still a large amount of video and audio tapes are dumped in the recording centers, theatres and with distributors of entertainment media. The history stored in the video tapes is still to be preserved since it contains vital information and has to be preserved according to the code of international standards. While it is very laudable step that is being taken by the institutions those who possess them in trust for the future generations. Yet it is an open question whether these attempts are proportionate to our large number of holdings in our various collections. The government of India sanctioned a project called National Manuscript Mission in the building where the IGNC is located. According to a report cited in the bibliography they have digitized about 20 thousand manuscripts as per a report of the NNM. However, all facilities at our command, at this point in time, are not enough and they need further strengthening. I think the project Director is no more in office these days for reasons better known to the Dept. of Culture Govt. of India.

It is true that we should not reduce our attempts in this direction to do full justice with the problems in hand. The fact of the matter is that even then we have organized the working facilities accordingly, yet some of this documentary heritage is still causing concern due to substantial disintegration of these originals. because of their vast magnitude. We are still very far from the complete care of these and a lot of conservation work still remains to be done. Keeping the idea of providing care to all our documentary heritage wherever they are, it is still very far from the reality and I am not sure whether full care would be possible to achieve with the in house facilities at our disposal. I do not advocate outsourcing agencies for this purpose unless there is strict control of the government directly or indirectly. These holdings are to be made open to public access and, therefore, it has to be provided to them in the public interest. The possibility of some damage can not be ruled out while handling them especially while handling the fragile documents.

One of the tried and tested way for this is using a Computer technology that enables Digitization of manuscripts wherever these are as a first aid measure till all manuscripts are provided preventive and curative conservation to them. The only difficulty in this regard is that most of our documentary heritage may not be able to bear digitization due to their fragile condition. We should ensure first that during digitization no damage happens to the original to add to the problems further. The original being authentic has it's own value and it has to be preserved at any cost. The fear is that the detailed curative conservation takes a long time to complete and, therefore, till then can we afford to wait, possibly no. During most of the time, the libraries, the archive collection and important records were in physical formats e.g. books, charts, maps, manuscripts, documents, photographs, newspapers and graphics etc.

Now with the new age of multimedia, Virtual reality, digital media, and world wide networking technology is a challenge for museums, libraries and archives including the film archives. After the introduction of media, films, sound recording, digital imaging, image data base computers, floppy disks,

CD-ROM's, web-site, e-mail, pen drive, hard Disks, flash Drives are well established. We learn why the digital photography and their preservation has become equally important today. Questions arising from the introduction of new imaging technology including photography, conservation and computer science. Due to the fast changing techniques and complex imaging technologies involved, the collection managers/Curators need well informed and realistic advice from the experts of Digital imaging well posted to help and create these results of the technology. Therefore, their number in very near future is going to surpass the number of our traditional heritage. Digitization, therefore, has assumed great importance to save our cultural holdings from disappearance from the seen for which we might have to repent, if proper action is not taken and sooner the better. In the mean time, we may create awareness among the Curators and collection in charges to physically conserve their holdings and do their digitization. So that we handle our originals to be cherished for ever. However, digitization done for viewing has also a self life but can be restored before it starts decaying. Digital simulation of faded colour photographs, Digital reconstruction of faded photographs, old movies by image processing can be done.

Chapter Six

PREVENTIVE CONSERVATION

Preventive conservation includes regular examination visits of the area wherever these manuscripts are stored. Periodic fumigation as a policy have to be planned before hand. Separation of those manuscripts which are in damaged condition have to be fumigated first followed by others which are in waiting. Dry brushing of the fumigated manuscripts by light brushing with a very soft brush or by a vacuum cleaner in which the suspended particles are collected in a bag attached with the cleaner on one side and water tank on the other side. Care has to be taken not to inflict damage to the manuscript. The particles of dust and the particulate material should not be allowed to contaminate other manuscripts. Good house keeping is a great help to keep away them to repel the micro-organisms and insects. The storage cases should be dust free and should be given insecticidal and fungicidal treatment before manuscripts are stored in them. The storage should have exhaust fans but the electric switches should be outside the storage so that the stagnant air atmosphere is free from it and there is a proper air circulation. Monitoring of the various parameters like temperature, RH, stagnant air and pollutant etc. should be made a regular exercise. We should have fire detectors installed in the storage or galleries. The monitoring has to be on regular basis. The manuscripts should have easy retrieval system to locate them.

Having made a complete study of the manuscripts and their deterioration and undertaking steps for conservation especially their Preventive Conservation are essential so that they do not decay in any way here after or retard the process of their deterioration. While the Curative Conservation is like a treatment in the hospital ward where the patient undergoes medical treatment including surgery and transplantation of damaged parts to restore the physical strength of the patient but before he is admitted in the hospital is kept in the observation ward. Where various tests are done to pin point the dearease he is kept under observation in the ICU. Where he/she is transferred to study would he/she improve before discharge. Preventive conservation helps the artifact to remain at least in it's present condition and it has to be maintained in perfect condition after treatment.

All the steps required for minimizing the threat of deterioration of the manuscripts in a collection as a whole to care for them well and is aimed to reduce the possible impact of various threats to the them even when they do not show any sign of damage. For total protection of manuscript repositories, Preventive conservation should be implemented prior to Curative conservation but it has to be followed after treatment as well. Under the present circumstances we should chalk out a scheme which is full proof to provide safety to the manuscripts. It should be implemented in three under mentioned stages:

(1) During Storage: since a major portion of the collections remains in the storage for most of their life. It is very essential that special and continued attention need to be paid to them for proper storage of these manuscripts remain without damage. Acid free and lignin free mount board boxes which are slightly bigger in size than the size of the individual leaves should be made. These should be stored in a specially made box which can be opened from one side to handle the manuscript without strain.

Manuscripts should be wrapped in insecticidal paper and then covered with a cotton cloth preferably of red colour. Thymol crystals in muslin cloth should be kept in the storage cabinet individual leaves and should not be tied in bundles. Every body should wear gloves while examining the manuscript or handling them by the curator for any purpose. The Stack area should be kept clean of dust etc. Insecticide and fungicidal spray should be done at intervals but it should be done after the removal of the manuscripts from them. No food should be allowed in these storage areas so that the rodents do not enter them. If need be we may put traps to take care of them.

2. During handling and transport: As their continuous handling, what to say of mishandling, it looks safe to use digitization, wherever possible so that the treated manuscripts and manuscript in good condition at least remain in good condition for easy access to the user but norms should be communicated to the users before hand, so that they donot put them in any undue stress. Hands should be dry,no pens and ball point should be allowed in the reserve collections and instead of it pencils are safe to use.

3. During Display: Special care has to be taken while displaying the manuscripts. The display cases should be fabricated from those materials which do not produce acidic or alkaline fumes. Proper light source like the optical lighting system to minimize the intensity of light and also is' duration. It is needless to say that maintenance of optimum temp. and RH conditions are to be insured. We should use acid free and lignin free tissue paper and boards of library standard as per international norms. No adhesive tapes and acidic glues to be used to reduce cost. One should know when to humidify and when to dehumidify according to parameters fixed on this view of point for a manuscript storage cases or display cases.

Preventive Conservation and Curative Conservation Comparison

Preventive Conservation Steps	**Curative Conservation steps**
1. It is carried out to reduce the rate of decay.	1. Carried out when some decay is noticed.
2. Entire collection can be attended at the same time.	2. One object or a part of it can be attended.
3. Cost effective method.	3. Costly process.

4. Specialized Laboratory not needed.	4. Specialized laboratory is needed.
5. Does not need costly tools & materials.	5. Requies sophisticated tools and materials.
6. Can be implemented by the Curators and the curatorid staff duty trained.	6. A trained Conservator is a must.

The Preventive measures can be a proactive treatment and is operational all the time, even though the collection does not suffer from any apparent damage and it's results may not be visible in comparison as compared to curative conservation. Many institutions having manuscripts in their collection are suffering due to lack of conservation infrastructure at various levels. Conservation is not only the responsibility of the conservation staff but is also the responsibility of the Curators and the collection In charges who are trained in their field of expertise. The government of India has created the National manuscript Mission for the purpose. They have to provide Preventive Conservation technology to many of such institutions as a first aid method so that the manuscripts can remain in good state of Preservation which are applicable to all manuscripts in the entire collection. It goes without saying that all manuscripts need these measures at least till the facilities for curative conservation are provided for the entire collection whether the manuscripts are in good state of Preservation or have decayed further due to the absence of proportionate curative conservation facilities till these are treated using latest technology of Curative Conservation. It however does not ensure that such objects which have been treated fully by all available technology at our command, would not decay any more unless preventive conservation measures also be continued here after.

One of the step that has to be taken care is that the objects which have been treated curatively have to be stored as well as have been displayed should go separately and should not be mixed with each other. The treated manuscripts, if not to be bound, should be kept in special acid free lignin free boxes with a flap system for opening them one over the other and to be picked while using gloves and should be handled carefully so as to use them safely. Unscientific repairs using tapes of any kind should be discarded since they not only look ugly but are producing harmful materials which decay the paper or other substratum. Many times unscientific repairs even hide the details of the manuscript and defeat the very purpose of the job. Use of iron clips and pins would further damage the manuscript leaves. Only acid free tissue paper to be used with starch paste. Periodic vacuuming would check the settling of these on manuscripts and future growth of biological agencies to damage them in future.

Besides the manuscript should be kept in controlled conditions of light, heat, relative humidity and dust free environment by adopting suitable methods of their protection, good housing keeping, proper handling and transportation from one place to the other in the institution or in other cities in India and abroad. These are simple and one does not need a scientist for this but scientific attitude. Here we can think of a Curator/ Conservator who would be available in all institutions and manuscript collection. Preventive measures for keeping the manuscripts in storage which is dust free and should be wrapped in acid free tissue or in a red starch free cotton cloth. The question is why red cloth? It is also for the fact that UV radiations can not reach the red cloth. The Spectrum of radiation from museum light source (day light, fluorescent and tungsten lamp) can be divided into three regions of wave length; ultra violet radiation (300-400nm), light or visible radiation (400-760nm) and infrared radiation beyond (760nm). UV & visible radiations of lower wave lengths than green can cause damage to manuscripts and library materials but the last three radiations including red do not reach the manuscript, thus the chances of damage are minimum. The attempt should be reduce both illumination and time of exposure.

Here I would like to emphasize that a Curator/Library In-charge would be available wherever a collection exists but there may not be any Scientific conservator in their institution. Our attempt should be have a conservation Unit with them but till this is achieved we should be able to provide Preventive conservation as prescribed above to help on the latest thinking on the subject for future generations to see, cherish and enjoy for all times to come. In the absence of AC we should use Art Sorb to keep the micro climate under control which should be neither too humid nor too dry which is not the ideal condition for them. The treated manuscripts also need preventive conservation. It is never the end but a beginning. When we also fall ill and take treatment to get well, but we should always take preventive measures so that we do not fall ill again. Conservation should be almost an integral part of all activities of a modern museum and gone are the days when some people in authority having different expertise, use to say I have no time for conservation. These words I had to swallow while in office, as an obedient government servant.

This attitude is dangerous for an all round development in a multi purpose museum. To me after an long innings of more than 50years in the profession still pinches me but I am happy that this attitude has changed over the years and we have started saying to our students that no museum can be termed a perfect museum with out conservation and restoration being the most essential activity to keep the collection so as to support the museum's other activities such as exhibition and interpret the collections of a museum which have been achieved by our generation after a very long and continuous efforts now for the enjoyment and education of our future generations for all times to come. The basic principles underlining Museum's conservation work are as follows. (1) Prevention (2) Reversibility and (3) Aesthetic responsibility. The most restorations are designed to be invisible to the naked eye. They take measures that the object looks complete while not observing the visual difference between original work and restorations. Badly damaged or inferior objects can have their individual value increased very considerably by suitable treatment. The degree of restoration that should be carried out on an object is to day a very contentious issue. Legitimate restoration of the kind that would be carried out in a museum and archives to achieve a balance where by the new work is clearly distinct from the original, whilst giving the overall impression of how the piece must been originally and how it is now looking. On the other hand fraudulent restoration seeks to hide any damage that exists. Museums and archives are required to have a set policy in this regard which should be very far from the Art dealers intentions to repaint or rewrite the manuscript to fetch more price without caring for authenticity of the work of art/document. We can not have the same policy in this regard as we may have in case of an traditional oil painting or a cotemporary Painting.

In conclusion I would like to say Research in conservation techniques is the answer. Conservation has two main aspects namely the research in conservation and the knowledge of materials by scientific study including identification of materials and the method of their fabrication. Similarly conservation also has two aspects actual conservation and preventive conservation which need updates in research for finding new methods which should include how the materials and techniques used in the past for conservation and restoration are to be evaluated so that the latest techniques could be researched to improve upon the techniques being used in conservation in general, in the interest of manuscripts and documents as the time moves on. Conservation preventive as well as curative is a continuous process and in no circumstances is, an one time activity since objects need inspection at intervals which should not have long gaps.

Chapter Seven

CONCLUSIONS

Although we can not say that a most ideal technique of conservation of manuscripts and documents has been found, however, in conservation of artifacts it is never fully ideal but very near to the most ideal since research has to be continued as new materials and equipments are adding on to the list of suitable techniques and equipments goes on and on. With the research continuing and it is an ongoing process, the attempt of the conservation scientists always is looking for the best in the interest of the ancient documentary heritage. A variety of methods have been developed which are suited to the different needs of individual Archives and museums, their workshops, and at the same time certain general principles have begun to emerge.

It is a fact that I have seen some specimen of paper documents having been laminated by the Indian method of lamination which after a few years were reported having problems of increase in acetic acid content resulting into charring and brittleness but we presume these were mostly not de acidified prior to lamination. I wonder not to comment in the absence of documention and records. Even then if research can guide us to find a solution, it would be fair enough. Lamination with a cellulose film under heat and pressure has been discarded by Indian conservators long ago. As an alternate the Morane process of lamination with the cellulose di or tri acetate coated with some un harmful adhesive at low heat and pressure could be thought off as some birch bark manuscripts were laminated by this process two-three decades back and are in good state. The advantage of this type of lamination is that the adhesive does get dissolved in alcohol and it does not affect the acetate film which is the case with the solvent lamination.

Adhesives are being developed these days which can be used for the dry mounting lamination which are expected to have a reasonable degree of permanence. The Post lip duplex process and the Dis pro process represent the new methods of lamination which have special features of using some logical method which is of interest and they merit further study as has been discussed already in detail. There is no doubt that further research will continue with a view to introduce new laminating films and adhesive that may be expected to lead to improved method of lamination. It is, therefore, desirable that National Research Laboratory for conservation of Cultural Property, Lucknow, The National Archives of India and the National Museum, New Delhi could associate with them being the other two National institutes in the field concerned.

BIBLIOGRAPHY

Abdel-Maksoud, G.M.M., Marcinkowska, E., 'Evaluation of vegetable tanned-leather after artificial ageing as compared to archaeological samples, ICOM Committee for Conservation, 12th Triennial Meeting, Lyon, (1990), pp.913.

Abduraheem, K.and Sheeba Khan, 'Integrated Methods for Safeguarding Archival Materials,' Conservation of Cultural Property in India, Vol.38 (2009), pp.61-64.

Abduraheem, K. and Sheeba Khan, 'Advance Methods for Preventive Conservation of Manuscripts', Conservation of Cultural Property in India, Vol.38 (2009), pp.149-152.

Arora, Anurag,' Digital Restoration, 'Conservation of Illustrated Manuscripts', Workshop Proceedings (Compiled by S.P. Singh, R.C. Jain and Vibhas Kumar), Organized by NMM, IGNCA and National Museum, New Delhi.

Catherine Sense, 'The Case Against Using Soluble Nylon in conservation work', Studies in Conservation, Vol.26, pp.102-110.

Cockerell, D.M., 'Bookbinding and care of Books', Sir Issac Pitman, London.

Agrawal, O.P., 'Conservation of Manuscripts and Paintings of South East Asia', Butterworths, London, 1984.

Agrawal, O.P. & Barkeshli, Mandana, 'Conservation of Books, Manuscripts and Paper Documents', INTACH Indian Council of Conservation Institute, Lucknow, 1997.

Agrawal, O.P. & Bisht, A.S., 'Non Aqueous Deacidification & Conservation of an Illustrated Manuscript Leaf' Conservation of Cultural Property in India (Prof. G.N.Pant Commemoration Volume), Ed. A.S.Bisht, I.K.Bhatnagar & S.P. Singh, Agam Kala Prakashan, Delhi-110052, pp.153-156.

Agrawal, O.P. and Bisht,A.S., 'Non Aqueous Deacidification and Preservation of an Illustrated Indian Manuscript Leaf', Studies in Museology, Vol.V, 1969, pp.34-37.

Agrawal (Ed) O.P., 'Conservation of Manuscripts & Documents' INTACH, Indian Conservation Institute, Lucknow.

Agrawal, O.P., 'Care and Preservation of museum objects,' NRLC, Lucknow (1977).

Agrawal, O.P., 'Preservation of Art objects and library Materials', National Book Trust, New Delhi, (1993)

Anurag Arora, 'Digital Restoration', Proceedings of a Workshop on Conservation of Illustrated Manuscripts, Organised by the NMM, IGNCA and the National Museum, New Delhi (15-19 March, 2010), pp.121-123.

Arai, H., 'On the Foxing Causing Fungi' IIC 8th Triennial Meeting, Sydney (1087), pp.1965-67.

Arai, H., 'Foxing Caused by Fungi: 25 Years of Study, 'Int. Biod. (2000), Vol.46: pp.181-188.

Baba, 'Ved Vahini', SSSBP Trust, Prasanti Nilayam, A.P.

Baba, 'Sathya Sai Speakes' Vol.III, pp.186-187.

Baba, 'Sathya Sai Speaks', Vol.VIII, pp.198-199.

Baba, 'Sathya Sai Speaks' Vol.VII, pp.107.

Baba, 'Upanishad Vahini' SSSBP Trust, (1981), Prasanti Nilayam.

Ballard, Mary,W. and Baer, Norbert S., 'Ethylene Oxide Fumigation: Results and Risk Assessment,' paper presented at Annual Meetingof the Society of American Archives, Washington, September 1984. Restaurator, Vol.7, pp.143-168.

Baynes, Cope A.D., 'The non –acqueous deacidification of Documents,' Restaurater, Vol.1, (1969), pp.2-9.

Baer, N.S. and Banks, P.N., 'Indoor Air Pollution: effects on Cultural and Historic Materials', The International journal Of Museum Management and Curatorship, (1985), Vol 4, pp.9-20.

Baer, N.S., Banks, P.N. 'Particulate Standards For Museums, Archives and Libraries', Presented at the 78th Annual Meeting of the Air Pollution Control Association, Detroit, Michigan, (June 1985).

Banik,G, 'Discolouration of Green Copper Pigments in Manuscripts and works of Graphic Art,' Restaurator, Vol.19, (1989).

Banik, G., Stachelberger, H. and Wachter, O., 'Investigation of the Destructive Action of Copper Pigments on Paper and Consequences for Conservation', Personal communication.

Barrow, W.J., 'Manuscripts and documents Their Deterioration and restoration,' University of Virginia Press, (1955).

Barrow, W.J., 'Poly vinyl acetate (PVA) adhesive for use in Library Book Bindings, Permanence/Durability of the Book IV' Richmond, Va(1965).

Barkeshli, Mandana, 'The Preparation of Copper Based Green Pigment (Zangar) in Iran as mentioned in Medieval Persian Texts,' Conservation of Cultural Property in India, Vol.29 (1996) pp.231-236.

Bayerr, G. and Wiedermann, H.G., 'Papyrus: the paper of Ancient Egypt' Analyt. Chem., Vol 55 (19830, pp.1220A- 30A.

Betty M. Haines, 'Minimizing Deterioration of Bookbindings leathers in Polluted Atmoshphers, in Guy Petherbridge', Conservation of Library and Archive Material and Graphic Arts', Butterworths Publication, pp.261-264.

Bhatacharya, A.K., 'Technique of Indian Paintings-A Study chiefly made on the basis of Silpa texts' Saraswat Library, Calcutta (1976).

Bisht, A.S., 'Blessings of Sai-My ultimate Goal' Book, published with courtesy of Agam Kala Prakashan, Ashok Vihar, Deep Market, Delhi-110052 for free distribution.

Bisht, A.S., 'Preservation of an Illustrated manuscript on Paper', Conservation in the Tropics, Proceedings of the Asia-Pacific Conference on Conservation of Cultural Property, Feb.1972, pp.96-102.

Bisht, A.S., 'Prevention and eradication of Biodeterioration in Museums-A Study of Problems and future Prospects,' Report presented at the VII Indo-US Workshop on Conservation held at Washington, May 1987.

Bisht, A.S., 'Digitization-A Technique to be used with caution for Preservation of Manuscripts', Conservation of Cultural Property in India, Vol.XXXVII (2007).

Bisht, A.S., 'Control of Biodeterioration in Museums-A Study of Problems' Biodeterioration of Cultural Property, Proceedings of the International Conference, Feb 20-25(1989) Lucknow, pp.98-103.

Bisht, A.S., 'Environmental Ethics-Linkages with Community & heritage.' Conservation of Cultural Property in India, Vol., pp.26-34.

Bisht,A.S., 'Conservation of Collection in Museum of national Importance- A Collective Responsibility' 'Museum Collection Concepts of Preventive Conservation, Proceedings of the National Seminar held at the Salarjung Museum, Hyderabad 18th-19th August 1997, pp.27-30.

Bisht,A.S., 'Project Restoration of some Ancient Artifacts in the Govt. Museum & Art Gallery, Chandigarh-A case Study', Conservation of Cultural Property in India, Vol.28 (1995), pp.72-77.

Bisht, A.S., 'Preventive Conservation of Archives and Library Holdings', The Indian Archives, Vol.XLIII, No.1-4.

Bisht, A.S., 'Preventive Conservation of Art Collections', The Glorious Heritage of India, (In Memory of Prof. R.C. Shrama) Editor: Dr. S.D. Trivedi, Vol.II, Agam Kala Prakashan, Delhi-110052, pp.433-438.

Bisht, A.S., 'Preventive Conservation is the Panacea for the study of Art Conservation,' Conservation of Cultural Property in India, Vol.38 (2009), pp.143-146.

Bisht, A.S., 'Repair and Restoration of Illuminated Manuscripts & Miniatures, Conservation of Traditional Records Paper and Allied Materials,' Proceedings of an International Seminar at New Delhi (1985), Organised by the S.W. Asian Regional Branch of the International Council of Archives, pp.125-131.

Bisht, A.S. 'Preservation of Illustrated Manuscripts & Miniatures Painted on both Sides,' Conservation of Cultural Property in India, Vol. IX(1976), pp.38-40.

Bisht,A.S., 'Prevention and eradication of Biodeterioration in Museums- A Study of Problems and Future Prospects', Journal of Indian Museums, Vol. XLIII (1987), pp.163-168.

Bisht, A.S., 'Ethics in Conservation-Problems and Prospects,' Conservation of Cultural Property in India, Vol.XXIII (1990), pp.17-22.

Bisht, A.S., 'Conservation Science' Book, Agam Kala Prakashan, Delhi (2003).

Bisht, A.S., 'Scientific Aspects Of Heritage Study, 'Book, Agam Kala Prakashan, Delhi (2004)

Bisht, A.S., 'Conservation of Indian Miniatures and Illustrated Manuscripts,' Book, Om Publications, New Delhi (2008).

Barrow,W.J., 'Amercan Archivist', Vol.VI, No.3 (1943), pp.151.

Barrow, W.J., 'Permanance /Durability of the Book, III', Spray Deacidification (1964), Richmond,Va.

Blank, M.G., Flyate, D.M., and Lotsmanova, E.M., 'The forecasting of the longevity of paper, Comparison of methods', ICOM Committee for Conservation Report 81/14/5,6th triennial meeting, Ottawa, (1981).

Boustead, W.M., 'The surface pH measurement and deacidification of Prints and drawings in Tropical climates', 'Studies in Conservation, Vol.9 No.2 (1964), pp.50-58.

Boustead, W., 'Conservation of Paintings and Graphic Art'. IIC Lisbon Congress (1972), pp.907-914.

Bridgman, C.F., 'Radiograpy of Paper', Studies in Conservation, Vol.10, No.1 (1965).

Chakravarti, S., 'A review of Lamination Process', Indian Archives, Vol,1 (1947), pp.304.

Choudhury, R.D., Jain, K.K. and Subhra devi, 'Traditional Preventive Conservation Practices of Assam with special reference to Sanchipat Manuscripts,' Conservation of Cultural Property in India, Vol.38 (2009), pp.104-108.

Darlington,I., 'The Lamination of Paper documents, an Interim Report on Methods available in U.K.', J.Soc. Archivist, Vol.1 No.4 (1956), pp.108.

Datta, P.K., 'Use of Neem Oil in Conservation' Conservation of Cultural Property in India, Vol.18-20 (1985-87), pp.98-100.

Dr.Perti(Ed), R.K., 'Conservation of Traditional Records Paper and allied Materials,' Proceedings of the International Seminar, New Delhi (December 16-19,1985), South and west Asian Regional Branch of the International Council on Archives (1987).

Das, Sudhir Kumar, 'Repair and Restoration of Parchment and Vellum Manuscripts' Conservation of Cultural Property in India,Vol.16-17 (1983-84), pp.161-163

Das, Sudhir Kumar, 'Repair and Restoration of Birch Bark Manuscripts', Conservation of Illustrated manuscripts, (Compiled by Shri S.P. Singh, R.C. Jain and Vibhash Kumar) Workshop Proceedings organized by NMM, IGNCA and National Museum, New Delhi (2010), 106-108.

Datta, Pankaj Kumar, 'Use of Neem Oil in Conservation', Conservation of Cultural Property in India, Vol. XVIII-XX(1985-87), pp.98-100.

Devi, Dhanpati L., 'Experiment on the Application of Artemisia Oil as Insecticide and insect repellant in the Museum' Conservation of Cultural Property in India, Vol.XXII (1989), pp.108-111.

Devi, H. Bilashini, 'Indigenous Practices for Preservation of Illustrated Manuscripts with special Reference to Subigya and Paphal Manuscripts,' Conservation of Cultural Property in India, Vol.38 (2009), pp.81-84.

Dhawan, Shashi and Agrawal, O.P., 'Fungul flora of miniature Paper Painting and Lithographs' Int. Biod.(1986), Vol.22, pp.95-99.

Dhar, S., 'Addressing cultural diversity challenges, meanings and consequence', 15th Triennial, ICOM, New Delhi pp. 1035-1040.

Farooqui, Anis, 'Art of India and Persia', B.R.Publishing Corporation, Delhi (1979).

Gairola,T.R., 'Preservation of some ancient Paintings and Manuscripts', Ancient India, Vol.8 (1952), pp.96.

Gairola,T.R., 'Handbook of Chemical Conservation of Museum Objects', Baroda University Press, Baroda(1959).

Gaurav, S.K.,Ferdosh Alam and Md. Nooruddin, A. 'Technical note on Conservation of Media Tapes,' Conservation of Cultural Property in India, Vol.38 (2009), pp.128-132.

Gear, J.L., American Archivist,Vol.21,(1958), pp.275.

Gilberg, Mark, 'Inert Atmosphere Disinfection Using Ageless Oxygen Scavanger' ICOM Committee For Conservation, Vol.II,1990, pp812-815.

Giri, S.V., 'Sai Upanishad (Ten Upanishads & Unpublished Vahini)', Sri Sathya Sai Sadhana Trust, Publication Division, Prasanti Nilayam, A.P. (March 2010).

Goswami, 'Descriptive Catalogue of Assamese Manuscripts', Rajguru, Medieval Assamese Society, pp.380.

Goel,O.P., Indian Archives, Vol.7(1953).

Goldthwait, John, 'A Practice for purifying the Heart', Book,s Sri Sathya Sai Books & Publications Trust, Prasanti Nilayam-515134.

Grattan, D.W. and Gilberg, M. 'Ageless Oxygen Absorber: Chemical and Physical Properties,' Studies In Conservation, Vol.39, No.3(1994), pp.210-214.

Gupta, K.K., 'Some Issues in the Conservation of Paper Material, with Special reference to Paper having Iron Gall Ink,' Conservation of Cultural Property in India, Vol.38 (2009), pp.48-53

Gupta.K.K., 'Conservation of photo Prints', Conservation of Cultural Property in India, Vol.11, (1978), pp.76-77.

Gupta,R.C., 'An Approach to Preservation of Photographic Materialos,' Conservation of Cultural Property in India, Vol.4(1969), pp.23-24.

H.Bilashani Devi, 'Indigenous Practices for Preservation of Illustrated Manuscripts with special reference to subigya and Paphal Manuscripts', Conservation of Cultural Property in India, Vol.38, (2009), pp.81-84.

Horie, C.V., 'Materials for Conservation,' Butterworths, London.

Hunter,D., 'Paper Making', The Gressel Press, London (1957).

Indictor, N., Baer, N.S. and Phelan, W.H., 'An Evaluation of Pastes for use in Paper Conservation' Restaurator, Vol.2, No.2(1975), pp.139-150.

Jain, Kamal K.(Editor), 'Conservation of Cultural Heritage (Essays in Honour of Shri A.S. Bisht), 'Agam Kala Prakashan, Delhi,(2009).

Janak singh, 'The Philosophy of the Rig Veda,' Sulabh India,Vol.22, August 2010, pp.23-26.

Jeevanandam, Malayappa, 'Sai Baba The Scientist, Compiled from Sai Literature', Book Vth Edition, June 2007.

Jeyraj,V. 'Care of Archival Materials' Book published by Tanjavur Maharaja Serfoji' Saraswati Mahal Library,' Thanjavur (1999), pp.58.

Jeyraj V. and Perumal, P. 'Indigenous Methods of Conservation of Manuscripts' Proceedings of the Workshop For training of the Trainers on Preventive Conservation of Manuscripts held at the Govt. Museum, Chennai,(2004).

Jeyraj, V., An Introduction to Digital Preservation, 'Conservation of Cultural Property in India,Vol.38(2009), pp.136-140.

Joel, A. Indictor, N., Hanlan, J.F. and Baer, N.S., 'The Measurement and significance of pH in Paper Conservation,' IIC-American Group Bulletin, Vol.1, No.2(1970) pp.119-125.

Jhonson, W. Arthur, 'A Practical Guide to Book repair and Conservation', Thames and Hudson, London (1998).

Kashliwal, K., 'Jain Granth Bhandars in Rajasthan', (1964), Jaipur, pp.2.

Kasturi, N., 'Sathya Sai Speaks,' Vol.vii, pp.299.

Kasturi, N., 'Loving God', Book, pp. 123-124,284-284 and 131,

Kasturi, N. (Ed.), Sanathana Sarathi, July 2000, pp.193-210.

Kharbade, B.V. and Agrawaql, K.C., 'Scientific Elucidation of Peacock Fethers believed to be used as Preservative for the Manuscripts' Concervation of cultural Property I IndiA, Vol.25 (1992), pp.99-108.

Kathpalia, Y.P. 'Conservation and Restoration of Archival Materials,' UNESCO, Paris(1973).

Kathpalia, Y.P., 'Care of Books in Libraries,' The Indian Archives, Vol.9, No.2(1956)

Kathpalia, Y.P., American Archivist, Vol.21 (19580), pp271.

Kishore, Ranbir, 'Preservation of National archives Assets-Present Status and Prospects' IASC, New Delhi.

Kuhn, H. 'Conservation and Restoration of Works of Art and Antiquities, Vol.1- 2, Butterwotths, London, pp.209-210.

Kharbade, B.V., Shrish Rajmalwar and Manjunathachari, R.C., 'An Application of Traditional Materials in Preventing Manuscripts from Biodeterioration,' Conservation of Cultural Property in India, Vol.38 (2000), pp.5-14.

Kharbade, B.V. & others, 'The use of Turmeric, a traditional Indian material in the presentational old manuscripts,' 15th Triennial ICOM, in New Delhi, pp 270.277.

Leledov,L.A., 'Professionl ethics in Restoration', ICOM Committee for conservation, 8th triennial Meeting Sydney, 1987, Vol.II, pp.545-548.

Lepeltier, Robert, 'Examination and Analysis of art Objects', The Restorer's Handbook of Drawings and Prints.

Mahurkar, Kamala, 'Conservation of Jain Kalpshutras', Conservation of Cultural Property in India, Vol.16-17 (1983), pp.56-58.

Marsh Frederick and Clare, Julian, 'A Conservation Method for Islamic Illuminated Manuscript Leaves', Conservation of Library and Archive Materials and Graphic Arts, Butterworths,(1987), pp.101-108.

Maran, Kite and Roy Thomson, 'Conservation of Leather and Related Mat erials', Butterworth-Heinemann, London (2004).

Mayer, Ralph, 'The Artist's Handbook of Materials,' Faber and Faber, London(1962).

Mehrnaz Azadi Boyaghchi, 'Scientific Elucidation For the Hanzal Extract reported to be used by Iranian Artists in Making old Paper Manuscripts', Conservation of Cultural Property in India,Vol.38, (2009), pp.1-4.

Mehra, C.P., 'Conservation of Cultural Property in India, Vol.6 (1973), pp.64-76.v

Mitra, Mallika, 'Conservation of an Illustrated Manuscript', ICCI, Newsletter, Special issue No.47, December, 2007, pp.19-20.

Morgan, W. Phillips, 'Notes on a method for consolidating Leather' JAIC1984, Vol.24, No.1.pp53-56.

Motichandra, 'An Illustrated Manuscript of Kalpsutra and Kalaa Chayakatha', Bulletin of the Prince of Wales Museum, Bombay, (1953-54), pp.40.

Naik, D.B. and Faleiro, Q.L., 'Use of Enzymes in paper Conservation-Our Experience', Conservation of Cultural Property in India, Vol, XXII (1989), pp.116-20

Nair, S,M., 'Biodeterioration of Paper', Conservation of Cultural Property in India,Vol.10,(1971), pp.22-28.

Nair, M.V. 'A New Method for relaxing Brittle Palm Leaves', Conservation of Cultural Property in India, Vol. 18-20, (1985-87), pp. 1-4.

Natham, Stolow, Conservation and Exhibitions' Butterworths, London.

Oddy, W.A., 'An Unsuspected Danger in Display', Museums Journal, Vol.73, No.1,(1973), pp.27-28.

Padhi, B.K., 'Preservation of Palm Leaf Manuscript in Orissa', Conservation of Cultural Property in India, Vol.VII,(1974), pp.62-65.

Perumal,P., 'Conservation of Palm Leaf Manuscripts', Studies in Art and Archaeological Conservation (Dr. B.B.Lal Commemoration Volume, Ed. A.S.Bisht and S.P.Singh), 2004, pp.1-8.

Petherbrige, Guy (Ed.), 'The Conservation of Library and Archive Materials and Graphic Arts,' Butterworths, London, 239-252.

Plenderleith, H.J. & Werner, A.E.A., 'The Conservation of Antiquties and Works of Art,' Oxford University Press, London(1966).

Plenderleith, H.J., 'Conservation of Prints, drawings and Documents', Oxford University Press, London.

Postlethwaite, Alan, W. 'Fumigation, Choice of fumigant and Design of Facility, Conservation, Analytical Laboratory, Smithsonian Institution, Wasihington, DC. Private communication after my visit to them.

Plumbe,W.J., 'The Preservation of Books' Oxford University, London (1964).

Prasad,Lalan Kumar, 'Role of Neem Leaves in Protecting Textile Materials and Paper Documents', Conservation of Cultural Property in India, Vol. XIV-XV (1981-82), pp.95-97.

Prajapati, C.L., 'Archivo Library Materials,' Mittal Publications (1997).

Prajapati, C.L., 'Conservation of Documents: Problems and solutions', Mittal publication, New Delhi(2005).

Press, R.E., 'Observation on the Foxing of Paper', International Biodeterioration Bulleitin, Vol.12 (1976), pp.27-30.

Pushpa, M.N., 'Plants used in the indigenous methods of Preventive Conservation of Manuscripts', Proceedings of the Workshop for training of the Trainers on Preventive Conservation of Manuscripts held at Govt. Museum, Chennai (2004).

Radhakrishnan, Dr. S., 'The Principal Upanishads', Books, Indus, New Delhi (1953).

Reed, R., 'Ancient Skins, Parchments and Leathers,' Seminar Press-London and New York,(1972), pp.13-23.

Rudolf Gschwind and Lukas Rosenthaler, 'The use of Digital Imaging for the preservation of the collections of Photographs and Motion Pictures', ICOM Committee for Conservation, 1996, Vol.II, pp.580-585.

Sadhu, A.R. and Mangiraj, V.R. 'Managing Pest Problems at ASI Circle Library, Aurangabad' Conservation of Cultural Property in India, Vol.38 (2009), pp.65-67.

Sarkar, N.N., 'Non-Chemical Methods in Library Management' Conservation of Cultural property in Indi, Vol.28(1955), pp.22-29.

Sharma, B.R.N., 'Pests and Pesticides in Archaeology and Archives,' Conservation of Cultural Property in India, (1992), pp.52-55.

Segal, Judith and Cooper David, 'The Use of Enzymes to Release Adhesives,' The Paper Conservation, Vol.2 (1977), pp.47-50.

Seetaharamaiah, D.N.V.S., 'Conservation and Preservation of Photographic Materials', Conservation of cultural Property in India, Vol.23 (1990), pp.30-34.

Seetharamaiah,D.N.V.S., 'Environment & It's Impact on Cultural Property : Photographic Materials', Conservation of Cultural Property in India, Vol.27, (1994), pp.42-44.

Senapati, S.K., 'Education in Preservation and conservation of Library Materials in India' Indian Library Association, Vol. XXIX, No.1-2, April-September (1993), pp.39-46.

Shridhar Andhare, 'Chronology of Mewar Paintngs', Agam Kala Prakashan, Delhi, 1987, pp.136.

Shaheen, Fauzia and Dhawan,Shashi, 'Natural Plant Products: A Safe Preventive Measure Against Anthrenus vorax (Coleoptrera: Doermestidal)', Biodeterioration of Cultural Property, Proceedings of the International Coference, 1989, Lucknow, pp.186-194.

Shah, U.P., 'Treasures of Jain Bhandars', L.D. Series, 69, Ahmedabad, 1978, pp .9.

Singh, R.S., 'Is De acidification Panacea to Conserve Paper,' Conservation of Cultural Property in India, Vol.32-33, (1999-2000), pp.101-105.

Singh, R.S., 'Conservation of Documents, in Libraries, Archives and Museums', Aditya Prakashan, New Delhi (1993).

Subhra Devi and Kamal K.Jain, 'Cleaning of Sanchipat Manuscripts: Need Re-assessment, Conservation of Cultural Property in India, Vol.38 (2009), pp.102-103.

Subhra Devi, Chaudhury, R.D. and Prof.Jain,K.K., 'Traditional Preventive Conservation Practices of Assam', Conservation of Cultural Heritage(Ed) Dr.K.K.Jain, (Essays in honour of Shri A.S.Bisht), 2000, pp.113-118.

Subhra Devi, and Prof.K.K.Jain, 'Some aspects of Conservation in Assam', Conservation of Cultural Heritage(Ed) Essays in honour of Shri A.S.Bisht, 2000, pp.107-112.

Soldatenkov, E.S., 'Computer in a restoration Workshop' Preprints ICOM committee for Conservation, 9th triennial Meeting Dresden (1990), pp.203-207.

Suman Kumari, R., 'Digital Preservation Initiatives of the Central Institute of Indian Languages(CIII), Mysore', Conservation of Cultural Property in India, Vol.38 (2009), pp.109-112.

Suri, J.H., 'Palm Leaf Manuscript in Jaisalmir', Indian Archives,Vol.1-2, 235–236.

Suryavanshi, D.G., 'Survey of Raw Materials in Old Paper and their role to Deteriorate the Art Objects,' Conservation Of Cultural Property in India,Vol.16-17(83-84),pp.131-134.

Shiva, Vandana and Holla-Bhar, Radha, 'Intellectual Piracy and the Neem Tree', The Ecologist,Vol.23, No.6, Nov.-Dec.1993, pp.223-227.

Singh, S.P., Jain, R.C. and Kumar, Vibhsh (Compiled by), 'Conservation of Illustrated Manuscripts,'(Published on the occasion of a Workshop held on the subject) by the IGNCA and NM, New Delhi, 2010.

Stolow, Nathan, 'Conservation and Exhibition: Packing, Transport, Storage, and Environmental considerations', Butterworths, London,1987.

Talwar,V.V., 'Restoration of Fragile Materials', Journal of the Madhya Prasdesh Itihas Parishad (1962).

Tandon, B.N., 'Problems in Conservation of Miniatures, Paper Paintings and Illustrated Documents,' Conservation of Cultural Property, Vol.10 (1997), pp.130-136.

Tandon,B.N., 'Scientific Investigation of a Jain Kalpsutra', Conservation of Cultural Property in India,Vol.VI (1973), pp.39-41.

Thomson Garry, 'The Museum Environment,' Butterworths, London, (1978).

Thomson,G., 'Recent Advances in Conservation', Butterworth, London.

Toishi, S.K. and Kenjo, T., 'Some aspects of the Conservation of Works of Art in Building of New Concrete,' Studies in Conservation, Vol.20 (1975), pp.118-122.

Uniyal,C.P., 'Technical Evaluation of Display and Storage Materials-A Vital Preventive Conservation Measures in Museums,'Proceedings of the National Seminar held at Salarjung Museum, Hyderabad, August (1997), pp.59-63.

Valentin, N and Preusser, 'Insect Control by Inert Gases in Museum, Archives and Libraries', Restaurator (1980)

Valentin, Nievos, 'Insect Eradication in Museums and Archives By Oxygen Replacement, A Pilot Project', ICOM Committee For Conservation,Vol.II, 1990, pp.821-825.

Vinas,V., 'The use of Polyetheylene Glycol in Restoration of Parchment in Guy Petherbridge's' Conservation of Guy Library and Archive Material and Graphic Arts' Butterworths Publication, pp.195-197.

VanSoest, H.A.B., T. Stambolov and Hallebeek, P.B., 'Conservation of Leather' Studies in Conservation, Vol.29 (1984), pp.21-31.

Vatsayan, Kapila, 'Miniature of Geeta Govinda,' Maharaja Sawai Mansingh II Museum, Jaipur(1980)

Ward, Philip, 'The nature of Conservation-a race against Time,' Book, the Getty conservation Institute, California.

Werner, A.E. 'The Lamination of Documents', A report presented to Joint Meeting of ICOM Committee for Museum Laboratories etc. Washington and Newyork, 17th Sept.-1st Oct., 1965.

Werner, A.E., 'Conservation and Display; Environmental control', Museums Journal, Vol.72, No.2 (19720,58-60.

Wilson, W.K., 'Deterioration and Preservation of Library Materials (Ed/H.W. Winger and R.D. Smith), The University of Chicago Press (1970), pp.174.

Waterer, John William, 'A Guide to the Conservation and Restoration of Objects made wholly or in part of Leather', 1973.

Waterer, J., 'A novel method for the conservation of fragile leathers', Studies in Conservation, Vol.17, pp.126-130.

Zaitseva, G.A., 'Protection of Museum Textiles and Leather against the Dermestid Beetle (Coleoptrera, Dermistidae) by means of antifeedants', Studies in Conservation, Vol.32, No.4(1987), pp.176-180.

INDEX

B

D

E

F

G

J

K

L

M

N

O

P

Q

R

S

T

U

V

Pl.1. The Papyrus manuscript in pieces from Egypt.

Pl.2. Palm leaf illustration (Nepal) showing traditional format.

Pl.3. Close up of the Illustration showing widespread loss of paint.

Pl.4. Wrong method of storing manuscripts.

Pl.5. Sanchi –pat manuscript leaf.

Pl. 6. Mandu Kalpsutra manuscript dated- C-1439 A.D.

Pl.7. Binding damaged very badly.

Pl.8. Illustrated manuscript showing faulty repairs.

Pl.9. Birch bark manuscript leaves showing faulty repairs (binding) with glue paste.

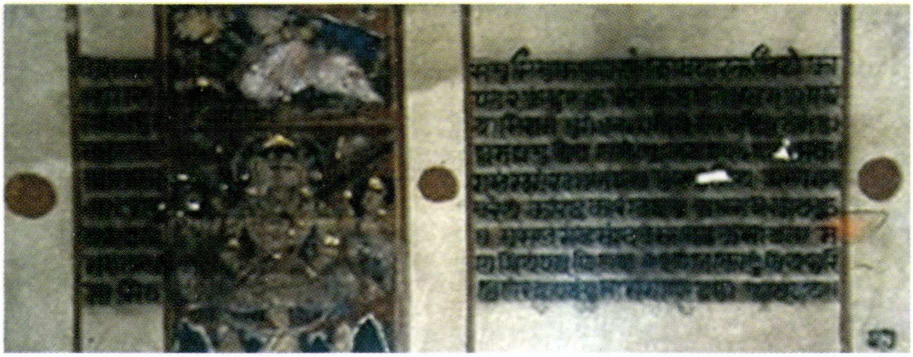

Pl.10. Manuscript leaf showing use of Acidic Iron Gall Ink.

Pl.11. Birch bark manuscript leaves showing damage and separation of layers.

Pl.12. Saha Nama manuscript leaf showing decay due to acid at the borders.

Pl.13. Persian manuscript showing ugly repairs to hide acid attack at the borders by verdigris.

Pl.14. Leather book binding eaten by insects/termites.

Pl. 15. Insect decay of Book Binding at the spine of an Arabic manuscript

Pl. 16. Book binding eaten by insects very badly starting from the spine to the leaves inside.

Pl. 17. Some bound books showing damage to them by insects.

Pl.18. Cellulose acetate lamination without proper de-acidification trapping the acid to grow within.

Pl.19. Palm leaf manuscript –tala showing dark stains due to handling with dirty hands.

Pl. 20. Illustrated Palm leaves -tala showing damages at the edges in general.

Pl.21. Palm leaf manuscripts (Sri Tala) damaged by separation of layers and the text.

Pl.22. Moghul Ramayana page badly repaired at the right side corners.

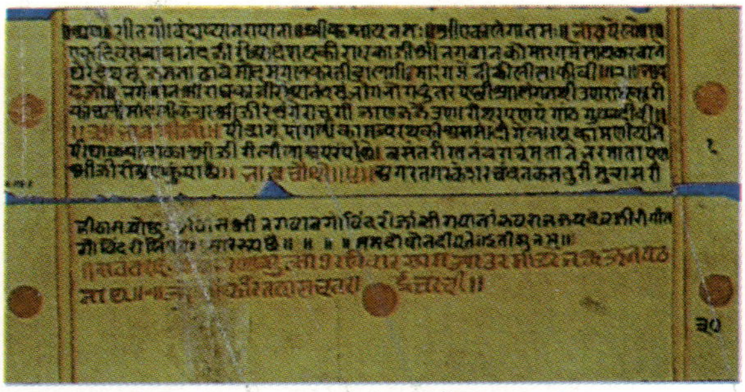

PL.23. Faking by over writing of Zawar Geet Govind manuscript.

Pl.24. Faking by repainting an old manuscript by Art dealers to fetch more price.

Pl.25. Birch Bark Leaf strengthened by giving a tissue paper backing.

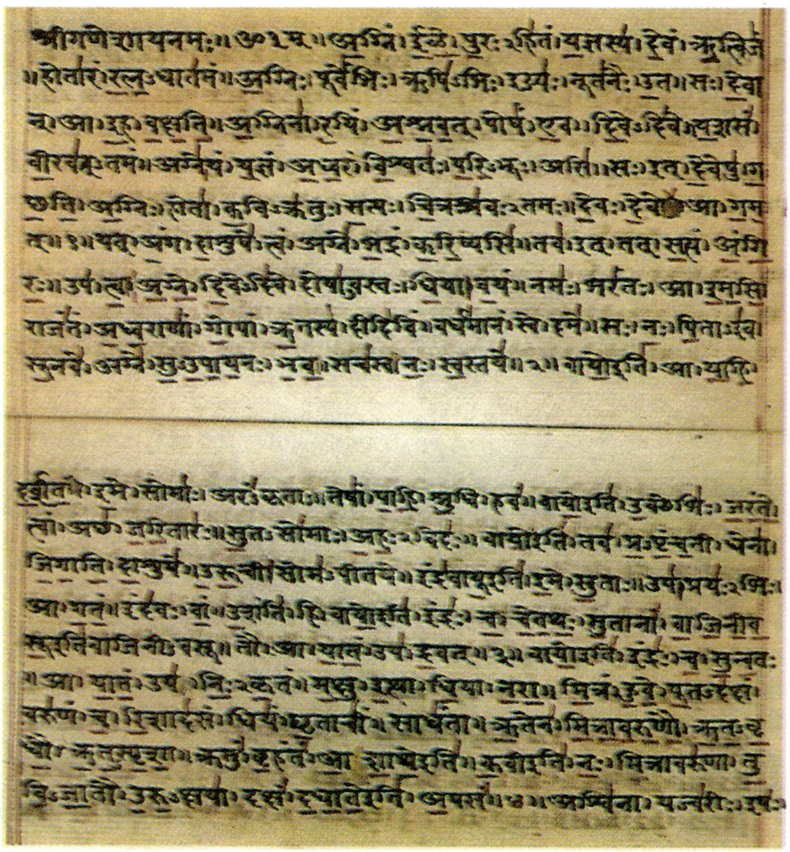

Pl.26. Very late copy of two pages of Rig Veda manuscript.

Pl. 27. Old manuscript badly eaten by termites and resulting into sticking of leaves.

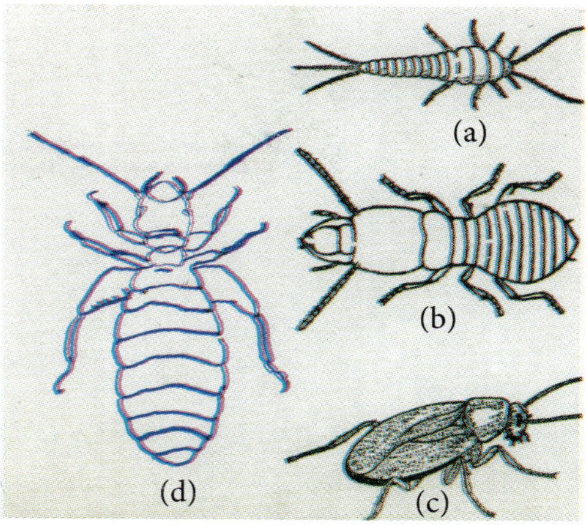

Pl.28. Some insects damaging manuscripts. (a) Silver fish (b) Termite (c) Cockroach (d) Book lice

Pl.29. Details of a manuscript leaf before restoration clearing the patchy repairs.

Pl.30. All old repairs have been removed showing the full text so far hidden after.

Pl.31. Damaged binding by loosening of threads & physical loss.

Pl.32. Binding damaged by insects.

Pl.33. Sanchi-pat manuscript as in stores before treatment.

Pl.34. Moghul Farman damaged by old repairs and wrong rolling.

Pl.35. Illustrated Manuscript leaf before conservation.

Pl. 36. Same Leaf after Conservation.

Pl.37. Old photograph before restoration.

Pl.38. Same after restoration.

Pl.39. Illustrated manuscript having faulty repairs after restoration.

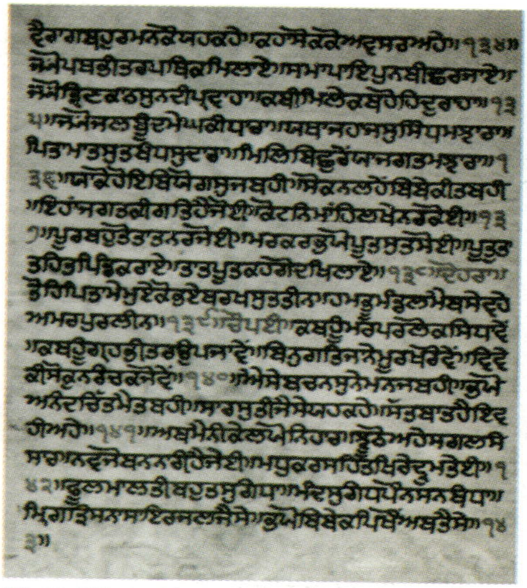

Pl.40. Wrong lining showing wrinkles which are uneven at the back.

Pl.41. Same Manuscript showing wrinkles, at the back.

Pl.42. Manuscript leaf stained covering the text.

Pl.43. Same after treatment making the full text visible.

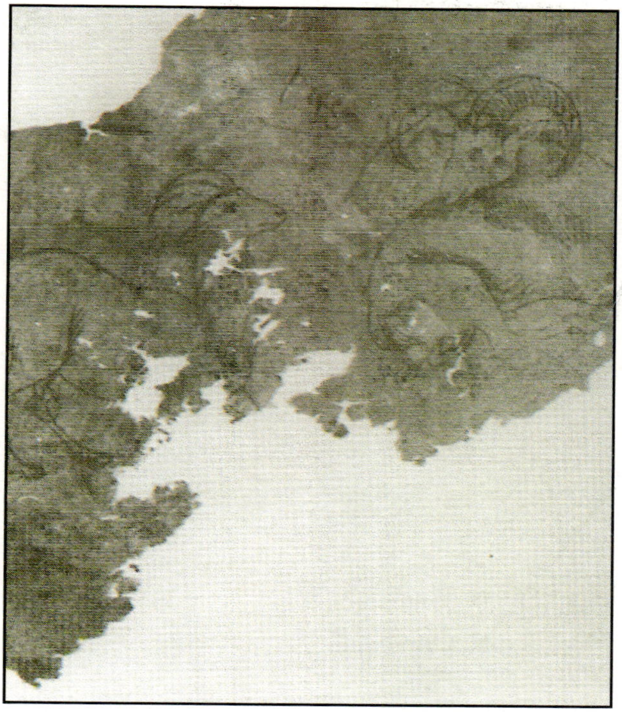

Fig. 44. Moghul drawing after treatment (Charba).

Pl. 45. Participants of the workshop sponsored by the N.M.M. with Authorities and the author.

Pl. 46. Author as the trainer of N.M.M. held at the National Museum with Former Director & Member Secretary of IGNCA.New Delhi.

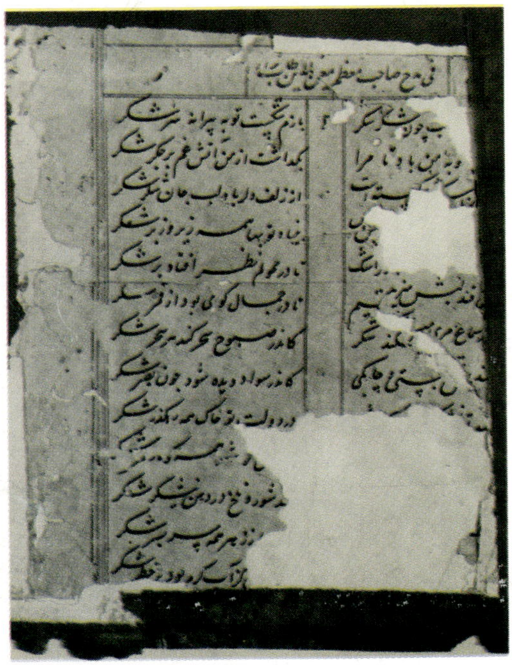

Pl. 47. Manuscript leaf in a damaged condition.

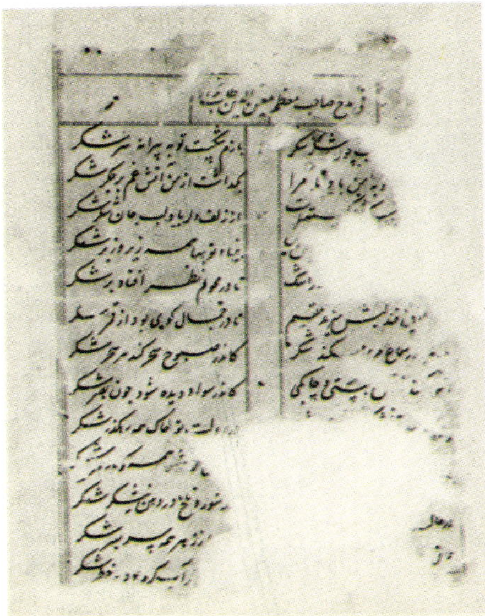

Pl. 48. Same after proper strengthening and lining.

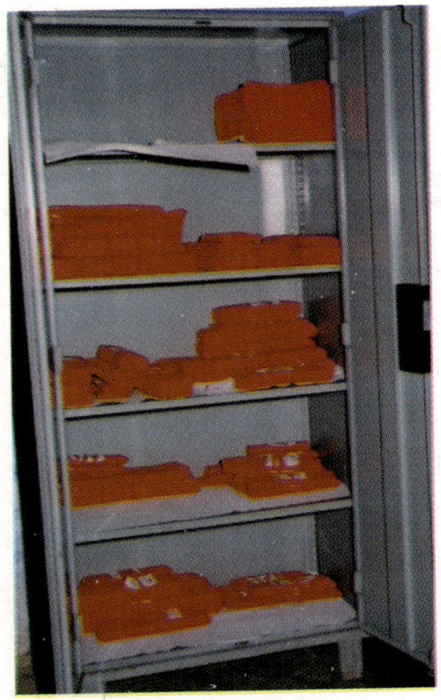

Pl. 49. Steel storage of treated manuscript wrapped in red cotton cloth.

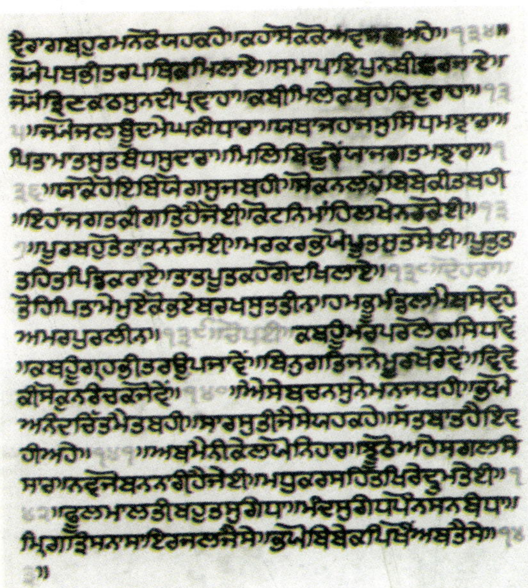

Pl. 50. Manuscript leaf after removal of the wrinkle and proper lining.

Pl.51. Saha-Nama manuscript leaf damaged by acid attack.